I0428841

Preface

This report is the 19th in a series of annual reports on recent trends in U.S. services trade that the U.S. International Trade Commission (the Commission or USITC) has published. The Commission also publishes an annual companion report on U.S. merchandise trade, *Shifts in U.S. Merchandise Trade*. These recurring reports are the product of an investigation instituted by the Commission in 1993 under section 332(b) of the Tariff Act of 1930.[1] The information contained in this report reflects the knowledge, industry contacts, and analytic skills that are used by the Commission in providing expert analyses of service industries in its statutory investigations and in apprising its customers of global industry trends, regional developments, and competitiveness issues.

In addition to the *Recent Trends* series, other recent Commission publications that include significant services content include *Digital Trade in the U.S. and Global Economies, Part 2,* and *Trade, Investment, and Industrial Policies in India: Effects on the U.S. Economy*. Moreover, within the past year several Commission staff members have published short studies known as Executive Briefings on Trade that focus on the services sector.[2] These include "Nigeria's Film Industry: Nollywood Looks to Expand Globally" (October 2014); "China's Trade and Investment in Financial Services with Africa" (October 2014); "Rwanda 'Leans In' to Information Services to Achieve Development Goals and Spur Competitiveness" (December 2014); "Kenya's Services Output and Exports Are among the Highest in Sub-Saharan Africa" (December 2014); and "Foreign Infrastructure Service Firms in Sub-Saharan Africa" (December 2014).

---

[1] On August 27, 1993, acting on its own motion under section 332(b) of the Tariff Act of 1930 (19 U.S.C. 1332(b)), the USITC instituted investigation no. 332-345, *Annual Reports on U.S. Trade Shifts in Selected Industries.* On December 20, 1994, the Commission on its own motion expanded the scope of this report to include more detailed coverage of service industries. Under the expanded scope, the Commission publishes two annual reports, *Shifts in U.S. Merchandise Trade* and *Recent Trends in U.S. Services Trade*. The USITC's current report format provides a systematic means of examining and assessing major trade developments, by product, and with leading U.S. trading partners, in the services, agriculture, and manufacturing sectors.

[2] The Commission's Executive Briefings on Trade are published at http://www.usitc.gov/research_and_analysis/executive_briefings.htm. These briefings are designed to inform the Commission and the public of current domestic and global activities that affect U.S. trade, investment, and competitiveness. They reflect the opinions and research of individual authors and are not the views of the Commission or any of its individual Commissioners.

Abstract

Recent Trends in U.S. Services Trade: 2015 Annual Report focuses on U.S. exports and imports of distribution services, including logistics, maritime transport, and retail services. In 2013, the United States exported $46.6 billion in distribution services, and imported $60.2 billion, resulting in a trade deficit of $13.6 billion in distribution services. U.S. distribution services contributed $2.3 trillion to U.S. gross domestic product (GDP) in 2013, or 17 percent of total U.S. private sector GDP. Distribution services employed nearly 23 million full-time equivalent employees in 2013, representing 21 percent of total U.S. private sector employment. However, during that year, average wages in all but one of the distribution services industries covered in this report (maritime transport services) were lower than the U.S. private sector average.

All three of the focus industries faced serious challenges as a result of the global economic recession of 2008–09. Since then, U.S. distribution services firms have had to adapt to a quickly evolving market that faces increased competition from new sources and growing domestic saturation. In addition, the spread of e-commerce has stimulated consumer demand for lower prices and faster, more flexible delivery, in turn affecting distribution services providers. Overall, as global economies become more integrated, U.S. distribution services industries will increasingly rely on burgeoning markets in developing countries to find new revenue streams.

Table of Contents

Tables

Acronyms and Abbreviations

3-D	three-dimensional
3PL	Third-party logistics (3PL)
4PL	Fourth-party logistics (4PL)
5PL	Fifth-party logistics (5PL)
ABP	Associated British Ports
APEC	Asia-Pacific Economic Cooperation
app	application
ASEAN	Association of Southeast Asian Nations
AU	African Union
B2B	business-to-business
B2C	business-to-consumer
BEA	Bureau of Economic Analysis
BRIC	Brazil, Russia, India, and China
BOT	build-operate-transfer
CAGR	compound annual growth rate
CMA CGM	Compagnie Maritime d'Affrètement and Compagnie Générale Maritime
COSCO	China Ocean Shipping Company
CSAV	Compañia Sudamericana de Vapores
CSCL	China Shipping Lines Container Co., Ltd.
dwt	deadweight tons
e-commerce	electronic (or online) commerce
e-tailers	electronic (or online) retailers
EU	European Union
FMC	Federal Maritime Commission
FTE	full-time equivalent
GATS	General Agreement on Trade in Services
GATT	General Agreement on Tariffs and Trade
GDP	gross domestic product
GPS	global positioning system
HPH	Hutchinson Port Holdings
ICT	information and communications technology
IMF	International Monetary Fund
IMO	International Maritime Organization
ISDS	investor-state dispute settlement
IT	information technology
ITU	International Telecommunications Union
M&A	mergers and acquisitions
m-commerce	mobile commerce (commerce via the use of mobile digital devices)

MSC	Mediterranean Shipping Co.
NAIC	National Association of Insurance Commissioners
NAICS	North American Industry Classification System
NOL	Neptune Orient Lines
OECD	Organisation for Economic Co-operation and Development
RMB	Chinese renminbi or yuan
SMEs	small and medium-sized enterprises
SOE	state-owned enterprise
SSA	sub-Saharan Africa
TEU	Twenty-foot equivalent unit
TISA	Trade in Services Agreement
TPP	Trans-Pacific Partnership
TTIP	Trans-Atlantic Trade and Investment Partnership
UAE	United Arab Emirates
UK	United Kingdom
UN	United Nations
UNCTAD	United Nations Conference on Trade and Development
USDOC	U.S. Department of Commerce
USITC	U.S. International Trade Commission
WCO	World Customs Organization
WTO	World Trade Organization

Executive Summary

The United States is the world's largest services market, and remained the largest global cross-border exporter and importer of services in 2013.[3] As in previous years, U.S. exports were highly competitive in the global services market—and their value was more than double the total of the next largest single-country exporter in 2013 (figure ES.1). Preliminary data for 2014 indicate that

Figure ES.1: The United States was the largest single-country exporter of commercial services in 2013

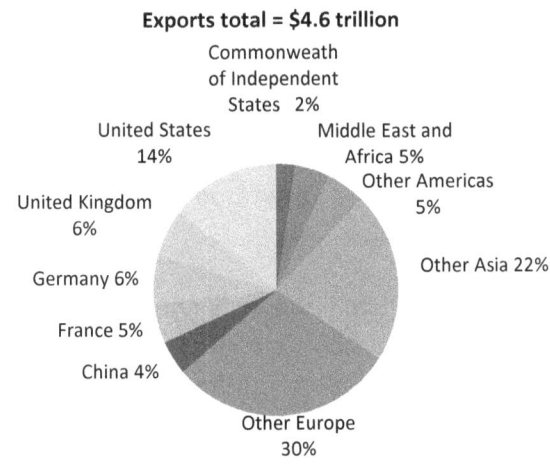

Exports total = $4.6 trillion

Commonweath of Independent States 2%

United States 14%

United Kingdom 6%

Germany 6%

France 5%

China 4%

Middle East and Africa 5%

Other Americas 5%

Other Asia 22%

Other Europe 30%

Source: WTO, *International Trade Statistics 2014*, 2014, tables A8 and A9.
Note: The term commercial services refers to private-sector services, and excludes public-sector transactions. Figures may not total to 100 percent due to rounding. The WTO includes the following countries under the Commonwealth of Independent States: Armenia, Azerbaijan, Belarus, Georgia, Kazakhstan, Kyrgyzstan, Moldova, Russia, Tajikistan, Turkmenistan, Ukraine, and Uzbekistan. (See appendix table B.1).

---

[3] This report uses time frames based on data availability—depending on the sources used, industry-level analyses may cover slightly different years. However, presentation of U.S. services trade data will largely remain consistent across the report. As of October 2014, BEA annual data on cross-border trade are available through 2013, while data on affiliate transactions are available only through 2012. Cross-border trade occurs when suppliers in one country sell services to consumers in another country, with people, information, or money crossing national boundaries in the process. Affiliate trade occurs when firms provide services to foreign consumers through affiliates established in the host (i.e., foreign) countries. For a more detailed description of the different modes of services trade, see box 1.1.

U.S. Services Trade Highlights

The United States continued to be the largest global exporter and importer of services in 2013. Distribution services (logistics, maritime transport, and retail services) made up a small but growing share of U.S. services trade.

Logistics services accounted for the majority of U.S. exports of distribution services in 2013, while maritime transport services led U.S. cross-border imports.

E-commerce, near-shoring, and digital technologies have increased demand for logistics services and are transforming the types of services that U.S and foreign logistics firms provide.

Maritime transport services are both highly regulated and highly globalized. In 2013, the United States posted a cross-border trade deficit in maritime transport services, largely due to the prevalence of foreign-based shipping firms.

The United States was the leading retail services market in 2014 (followed by China) and home to the largest global retailing firms.

U.S. services exports exceeded those in 2013 by 3.4 percent, or $22.7 billion, whereas U.S. imports were 4.1 percent higher ($7.7 billion) in 2014 than in 2013.

The *2015 Recent Trends in U.S. Services Trade* report, part of an annual series prepared by the U.S. International Trade Commission (Commission or USITC), provides an overview of U.S. trade in services. This year's report focuses on recent developments in three distribution services industries:[4] logistics, maritime transport, and retail services.[5] Distribution services firms perform a critical role in modern market economies by connecting manufacturers to consumers.[6] Generally, an efficient distribution services sector supports economic development, improves overall economic welfare, and is associated with domestic and international market integration. Distribution services can also enhance the liberalization of trade by allowing consumers to access a diverse array of products at lower prices. However, when operating inefficiently, distribution services can result in misallocated resources and higher costs throughout the supply chain.

Since trade in distribution services is driven by consumer demand, fluctuations in income and consumer spending can have profound effects on the health of the industry. For example, the global economic recession of 2008–09 caused revenue declines for the majority of distribution services providers. Further, as global economies become more integrated, the distribution services industry has needed to evolve rapidly to address issues such as shifting global supply chains, advances in digital technology, and increasing cost competition across all factors of production and distribution.

Distribution services providers have grown more "adaptive" as supply chains compress and e-commerce activity rises (figure ES.2). Manufacturers of both intermediate and final goods are increasingly moving their production processes closer to their target markets ("near-shoring")—usually to cut transportation costs and increase supply chain flexibility. In the same vein, with the growing use of Internet technologies to purchase goods, consumers have also increased demand for two-day and even same-day shipping for more products. Hence, demand for shorter delivery time frames across the distribution services supply chain has required logistics,

---

[4] Beginning with its publication in 2013, *Recent Trends* covers three industries per year, rotating on a four-year basis between professional services (education, healthcare, and legal or management consulting services); electronic services (audiovisual, computer, and telecommunication services); distribution services (logistics, retail, and transportation services (maritime transport)); and financial services (banking, insurance, and securities or leasing services). The 2014 *Recent Trends* report focused on electronic services.

[5] Logistics services include freight forwarding; freight transport by air, road, or rail; warehousing and storage; tracking and tracing; and customs brokerage; as well as value-added services such as supply chain and inventory management. Maritime transport services include maritime freight transport and port services. Retail services include general merchandise stores; stores specializing in specific merchandise categories (e.g., electronics and clothing); and non-store retailers (e.g., telemarketers and online retailers). For a more detailed description of each of these services industries and available trade data, see boxes 3.2, 4.3, and 5.2.

[6] Wholesale and retail services firms form the core of the distribution services industry, while logistics and transportation services companies provide the vital link between manufacturer, wholesaler, retailer, and final consumer. For an illustration of how the distribution services supply chain is organized see figure ES.2. Although wholesale services was not given a separate chapter, this report's definition of "distribution services" does include wholesaling, reflecting BEA trade data categories.

Figure ES. 2: Distribution services supply chain: Technology has increasingly enabled manufacturers to bypass traditional wholesalers and retailers

Source: Compiled by USITC.

transportation, and retail services firms to better coordinate transport routes and streamline inventory management.

Lastly, firms are facing greater competition from companies both within and outside the industry. For instance, small and medium-sized manufacturers often ship goods directly to consumers, bypassing traditional retailers entirely. Increasing competition has limited the ability of many distribution services companies to raise (or even maintain) prices. Consequently, a growing number of distribution services firms have focused instead on protecting profits by introducing new services and/or reducing internal costs and increasing the efficiency of operations throughout the supply chain—often adopting innovative digital technologies to do so.

Key Findings

Total U.S. Trade in Services

The United States was the leading global services supplier in 2012–13

Services accounted for $10.6 trillion (78 percent) of U.S. private sector gross domestic product (GDP) in 2013, and for 87 million (82 percent) of private sector employees. The United States remains the world's leading single-country exporter and importer of services. In 2013, U.S. commercial services exports totaled $662.1 billion, and accounted for 14 percent of global cross-border exports, while U.S. imports were $431.5 billion and accounted for 10 percent of global imports. The United States had a trade surplus of $230.5 billion. Other top single-country services exporters were the United Kingdom and Germany, each accounting for 6 percent of the global total.

As in previous years, travel services and passenger fares accounted for the largest share of U.S. services trade in 2013, representing 32 percent of exports and 31 percent of imports. Distribution services accounted for 7 percent ($46.6 billion) of exports and 14 percent ($60.2 billion) of imports in 2013, resulting in a trade deficit of $13.6 billion in this sector for 2013.

Services (including distribution) supplied by U.S.-owned foreign affiliates, the leading channel by which many U.S. services are delivered to foreign markets, increased by 3.7 percent to nearly $1.3 trillion in 2012. Distribution services[7] led affiliate sales, accounting for $399.0 billion or 31 percent of total services covered in this report. In 2012, top markets for sales by U.S.-owned affiliates were the United Kingdom (15 percent), Canada (10 percent), and Japan and Ireland (6 percent each). On the other hand, purchases from U.S. affiliates of foreign firms were $802.0 billion in 2012, an increase of 2.6 percent from the previous year. Germany and Japan supplied the largest share of such services (15 percent each). Overall, 53 percent of these services were purchased from foreign-owned affiliates of firms based in the European Union (EU).

Distribution Services

Logistics services accounted for the majority of U.S. cross-border trade in distribution services in 2013

As mentioned, in 2013, U.S. cross-border exports of distribution services totaled $46.6 billion, whereas imports totaled $60.2 billion, resulting in a trade deficit of $13.6 billion. Logistics services (including air freight and airport services) represented 51 percent ($23.9 billion) of total U.S. distribution services exports and 36.8 percent ($17.2 billion) of imports in 2013.[8] Maritime transport services (including both maritime freight and port services) accounted for 36.8 percent ($17.2 billion) of distribution services exports and 65 percent ($36.3 billion) of imports. In 2013, the top three markets for U.S. exports of logistics services were the United Kingdom (17 percent), Germany (7 percent), and Japan (6 percent). The leading markets for U.S. exports of maritime transport services were Japan (13 percent), Taiwan (9 percent), and Germany (8 percent).

---

[7] BEA data on affiliate transactions in distribution services specifically include data on wholesale, retail, and transportation and warehousing services.

[8] This report uses BEA data on air freight and airport services to discuss U.S. trade in logistics services. However, the report's qualitative discussion of the logistics services incorporates a broader definition of the sector. That includes activities such as freight forwarding, multimodal transport, warehousing and storage, and customs brokerage, among others. See chapter 3, "Logistics Services," 65.

Affiliate transactions accounted for the majority of distribution services trade in 2012

The majority of U.S. distribution services trade occurred through affiliate transactions. As mentioned previously, affiliates of U.S. distribution services companies located abroad (U.S.-owned foreign affiliates) represented the largest share (31 percent or about $399.0 billion) of covered services supplied by U.S. affiliates abroad in 2012. Within distribution services, wholesale trade accounted for the majority of services supplied by U.S. affiliates abroad (60 percent). Retail trade also accounted for a significant share (25 percent) of sales by U.S.-owned foreign affiliates, reaching nearly $101.0 billion in 2012. By contrast, the value of distribution services purchased from foreign-owned U.S. affiliates (i.e., affiliates of foreign firms located in the United States) was $235.0 billion in 2012. Wholesale trade accounted for the largest share (60 percent) of purchases from foreign-owned U.S. affiliates, totaling $142.0 billion, whereas retail trade accounted for 19 percent of such purchases.

Distribution services' GDP contribution and wages grew in 2013, but employment experienced a modest decline

In 2013, the contribution of U.S. private sector distribution services to U.S. gross domestic product (GDP) grew by 1.7 percent to $2.3 trillion, accounting for nearly 17 percent of total U.S. GDP. Among the distribution services industries, maritime transport services' share of GDP grew the fastest in 2013 at 9.4 percent, followed by retail trade (2.4 percent), wholesale trade (1.6 percent), and logistics services (1 percent). Overall, wholesale and retail trade each represented about 40 percent of distribution services' contribution to U.S. private sector GDP in 2013, followed by logistics services (18 percent) and maritime transport services (1 percent).

In 2013, distribution services employed 23 million full-time equivalent (FTE) employees, or more than 20 percent of the total U.S. private sector workforce. Retail services employed nearly 13 million people, accounting for 57 percent of total distribution services employment, followed by wholesale services (24 percent) and logistics services (18 percent) (figure ES.2). However, the number of FTEs in the distribution services sector fell at an annual rate of about 1 percent between 2008 and 2012, resulting in the loss of slightly more than 1 million FTEs.

Within the distribution services sector, the average annual output per worker varied widely by industry, ranging from $69,032 in the labor-intensive retail services industry to $296,825 in the capital-intensive maritime transport services industry.[9] At the same time, workers in the distribution services sector earned $46,671, on average, in 2013. This represented a 1.1 percent increase from the previous year, but was lower than the private sector average of $56,554. Like labor productivity, average wages in the distribution services sector covered a wide range— from $33,522 in retail services to $84,372 in maritime transport services.

---

[9] To illustrate, the value of output per worker in the maritime transport services industry is likely higher as a result of investments in new technologies and infrastructure to handle cargo more efficiently. U.S. port services firms are also investing in automation as part of an effort to control labor costs in order to maintain competitiveness.

Logistics Services

The United States was the largest global logistics provider by revenue in 2013

In 2013, the United States was the largest global provider of third-party logistics (3PL) services (a key segment of the logistics sector), accounting for nearly 21 percent of global logistics revenue. China and Japan ranked second and third, with market shares of roughly 18 percent and 9 percent, respectively. Among the top 10 markets for 3PL services, China recorded the largest revenue increase in 2013 at 7.6 percent, followed by India (4.8 percent) and the United States (3.2 percent). Market concentration has been declining: during 2013 the top 10 global 3PL firms accounted for roughly 20 percent of global market revenues, down from almost 30 percent in 2008. Germany-based DHL Global Supply Chain and Global Forwarding posted the largest revenue share at 4.5 percent, whereas U.S.-based C. H. Robinson Worldwide accounted for less than 2 percent of global logistics revenue in 2013 and ranked fifth worldwide. C.H. Robinson was the only U.S. firm to place among the top 10 global logistics firms in 2013. Overall, revenue of the top 10 3PL firms has been stagnant or declining since 2008, in part due to a decrease in freight volumes. Continued growth in global merchandise trade in response to improving economic conditions will likely have a strong impact on the logistics industry.

U.S. exports of logistics services increased by 7.0 percent to a high of $23.9 billion in 2013, while sales by U.S.-owned foreign affiliates grew strongly during 2008–12

In 2013, the U.S. surplus in logistics services rose by about 28 percent from 2012—a significant gain, though slower than the 40 percent increase recorded during 2011–12. U.S. cross-border exports of logistics services grew at an annual rate of only 0.5 percent during 2008–12, but rose by 7.0 percent in 2013 to reach a high of $23.9 billion. The United Kingdom was the largest single U.S. export market for logistics services in 2013, accounting for 17 percent of U.S. exports in the sector. Other major export markets for U.S. logistics services were Germany (7 percent), Japan (6 percent), China (5 percent), and Brazil (4 percent). By contrast with cross-border exports, sales by U.S.-owned foreign affiliates grew at an annual rate of nearly 21 percent between 2008 and 2012, reaching their highest level in 2011 at $20.1 billion. Although U.S. cross-border exports of logistics services exceeded sales by U.S.-owned foreign affiliates during this period, sales by U.S-owned foreign affiliates grew faster. This may suggest that U.S. logistics firms are responding to a growing demand for value-added services (e.g., inventory management and order fulfillment) that are more efficiently provided through a commercial presence.

Maritime Transport Services

The global maritime transport services industry comprises large container shipping and port services firms, many resulting from mergers and acquisitions

In 2013, the top 10 container shipping lines accounted for a 60 percent share of global container carrying capacity. The 10 leaders' total revenue of approximately $110.0 billion that year represented a 4.7 percent decrease from the previous year and contrasted with annual growth of 0.9 percent during the 2008–12 period. The composition of the top 10 global shipping firms continues to evolve, as companies have either merged with or acquired other large maritime firms in order to combine shipping assets and extend transit routes. Four of the top 10 global shipping firms—Maersk, COSCO, Evergreen, and Hanjin—also serve as port terminal operators. These four firms were formed through a combination of corporatization,[10] merger and acquisition, and global network expansion, much of which occurred as part of a wider trend towards port reform. The maritime transport services industry will continue to be affected by changes in global supply chains, an increase in shipping capacity with the deployment of ever-larger container ships, and the consolidation of service suppliers through global alliances.

In 2013, the United States posted a cross-border trade deficit in maritime transport services, largely due to the prevalence of foreign-based shipping firms

In 2013, U.S. exports of maritime transport services reached $17.2 billion, and U.S. imports totaled $36.3 billion, resulting in a U.S. trade deficit in this sector of $19.1 billion. The deficit reflects the fact that most U.S. imports and exports are conveyed on foreign vessels. The top five countries receiving U.S. exports of maritime transport services in 2013 were, in descending order, Japan, Taiwan, Germany, South Korea, and China. The United States posted trade deficits with each of these countries, the largest of which was with Japan ($2.9 billion). In 2012, total sales of maritime transport services by U.S.-owned foreign affiliates were $8.7 billion, down 4.4 percent from 2011. By comparison, total sales by foreign-owned U.S. affiliates in 2012 reached $6.5 billion. While this was an increase of only 1.1 percent from the previous year, these sales grew at an average annual rate of nearly 28 percent during 2008–11. The large growth in the value of foreign-owned U.S. affiliate sales partly reflects an increase in rates and volume of maritime freight between 2009 and 2010, as well as gradually improving global economic conditions.

---

[10] Under corporatization, a statutory port authority becomes, by law, a government-owned corporation, and most commercial port services are then provided by private entities. For further discussion, see box 4.1.

Retail Services

The United States was the leading retail services market in 2014 and home to the largest global retailing firms[11]

In 2014, global retail sales revenue reached $19.7 trillion, an increase of 22.4 percent from 2010. The United States was the world's largest retail market in 2014, with revenue totaling $3.7 trillion, or 18.7 percent of the global total. The U.S. market share of global retail revenue was largely unchanged during 2010–14, primarily due to the strength of the dollar, while the share of the G7 group of industrialized countries[12] fell from 43 percent of global retail revenue in 2010 to 38.5 percent in 2014. By contrast, the BRIC countries (Brazil, Russia, India, and China) grew to account for 27 percent of the global retail revenue in 2014, up from 22.6 percent in 2010. China, the world's second-largest retail market, experienced the largest revenue growth between 2010 and 2014; China's retail revenue increased by 4.4 percent to $2.9 trillion in 2014. Industry analysts forecast positive growth in global retail markets in the coming years.

The world's top 10 retail firms in 2012 were based in the United States or Europe (according to the latest available comparative data). Five of the leading 10 firms were headquartered in the United States, and all but one of these generated sales revenue outside the United States. The overwhelming global retail leader was U.S.-based Walmart, which operates in 28 countries and generated total revenues of nearly a half-trillion dollars in 2012. Walmart is more than four times the size of the second-largest global retailer, UK-based Tesco. Eight of the world's top 15 retailers derived over 50 percent of their sales revenue outside their home country, operating on average in 18 foreign markets.

In 2012, U.S.-owned foreign affiliates in retail services posted strong annual sales growth, reflecting rebounding consumer merchandise spending since the global recession of 2008–09

In 2012, U.S.-owned foreign affiliates supplied $101.0 billion in retail services. This represented an increase of 10.3 percent over the previous year and contributed to average annual growth of 12.2 percent since 2008. Strong U.S. affiliate sales during the period reflect increased consumer spending, as economies continued to recover from the global recession of 2008–09. Leading markets for U.S.-owned retail affiliates in 2012 are also major U.S. trading partners. Canada was

---

[11] Retail establishments include businesses that sell merchandise, such as motor vehicles, furniture, electronics, building materials, clothing, sporting goods, as well as food and beverages (including grocery stores but not restuarants).

[12] Canada, France, Germany, Italy, Japan, the United Kingdom, and the United States.

the top market, accounting for 24 percent of the sector's affiliate sales, followed by the United Kingdom (18 percent), Mexico (9 percent), Germany (7 percent), and Japan (6 percent).

Although cross-border sales via e-commerce are increasing, the majority of U.S. retail sales outside the United States are through foreign affiliates of U.S. retailers. Moreover, growth in U.S. firms' foreign affiliate sales has outpaced that of domestic sales, and U.S. retailers are increasingly looking to foreign markets to boost sales revenues and profits. In China, the world's second-largest and fastest-growing global retail market, U.S. affiliate sales reached $4.1 billion in 2012, up from $2.4 billion in 2009.

Foreign firms' retail affiliates in the United States supplied $43.7 billion of retail services in 2012. This was an increase of 6 percent over 2011, in line with an average annual growth rate of 6.5 percent since 2008. U.S. affiliates of Europe-based retailers accounted for two-thirds of the sales of U.S. affiliates of foreign firms in 2012. Many of these European retailers operate leading grocery businesses in the United States.

Recent USITC Roundtable Discussion

The Commission hosted its eighth annual Services Roundtable on October 16, 2014, with Chairman Meredith Broadbent and Commissioner Rhonda Schmidtlein moderating. The Commission regularly holds these roundtables to encourage discussion among individuals from government, industry, and academia about important issues affecting services trade. This year's event focused on services trade in sub-Saharan Africa (SSA), ongoing international trade in services negotiations, and the assessment of services commitments.

During the first half of the roundtable, participants discussed the prospects for growth in certain SSA services sectors; lingering challenges to and potential solutions for increasing services trade in various SSA countries; and the effects of China's growing investment and commercial presence in the region. Participants noted that several services industries in SSA have experienced rapid growth in recent years, particularly in the financial, telecommunications, and retail services sectors. Participants highlighted that rapid development of wireless telecommunications infrastructure in the region has increased trade in a wide range of services through the growing use of mobile digital technologies—including the provision of insurance, education, and healthcare services. Also, improvements in transportation networks and other distribution services have lowered transaction costs and opened the possibility for greater retail services trade. However, continuing challenges relating to lack of infrastructure and legal and regulatory enforcement continue to hamper services exports in many SSA countries. Nonetheless, participants were encouraged by increasing international initiatives (both public and private) that support cooperation and regulatory capacity building, and the growing recognition by SSA government policy makers of the importance of services trade development.

Participants also discussed the effects of increased investment by Chinese state-owned enterprises (SOEs) on U.S. and international commercial interests in the region. Participants acknowledged that Chinese views, particularly on how to regulate certain industries, have become more influential in several SSA countries. Participants saw this influence likely growing in the future, and suggested that it would be beneficial for the United States to work with China on building transparent regulatory institutions and enhancing the rule of law in SSA.

During the second half of the roundtable, participants considered several issues surrounding ongoing international trade negotiations relating to services—the Trans-Pacific Partnership (TPP) agreement, the Trans-Atlantic Trade and Investment Partnership (TTIP) agreement, and the Trade in Services Agreement (TISA). Beginning with an overview of the state of current services negotiations at the World Trade Organization (WTO), participants then discussed how potential TPP, TTIP, and TISA commitments would affect certain industries. The participants focused on three cross-cutting services issues—localization measures and freedom of cross-border data flows; rules that require SOEs to compete on an equal footing with private companies; and the development of ways to reduce costs associated with resolving differing industry regulations and standards. Most participants agreed that limiting transnational data flows would negatively affect a wide range of services industries, inside and outside of the information and communications technology sector. Further, participants noted the importance of disciplines regarding SOEs in the TPP, which should require them to compete on a level playing field with private firms and not benefit from subsidies or government financial support. Lastly, the majority of participants agreed that future agreements should look to establish a cooperative mechanism to efficiently develop solutions to regulatory differences, and affirmed that once concluded, current services-related negotiations may serve as a framework for further progress at the WTO.

Chapter 1
Introduction

Services continue to be a growing and important sector in the U.S. economy. The United States remains the world's top exporter and importer of private services, while the service sector accounted for 78 percent of U.S. gross domestic product (GDP) and 82 percent of employment in 2013. The World Trade Organization (WTO) reports that the U.S. services trade surplus in 2013 ($230.5 billion) was the world's largest, followed by that of the United Kingdom ($118.7 billion).[13]

This annual report examines U.S. services trade, highlights important U.S. trading partners, and analyzes global market conditions in selected industries. It focuses on the distribution services sector, particularly the logistics services, maritime transport services, and retail services industries.[14] In 2013 distribution services employed nearly 23 million people, represented 14 percent of GDP, and grew 1.7 percent from 2012.[15]

Data and Organization

The U.S. International Trade Commission (Commission or USITC) draws much of the services trade data used throughout this report from the Bureau of Economic Analysis (BEA) in the U.S. Department of Commerce (USDOC). The BEA collects services trade data through a number of surveys, which under most conditions require respondents with more than $2 million in exports or $1 million in imports to furnish details about their international services transactions. The BEA estimates trade flow data using these survey results.[16] This year, the BEA has updated its services trade data to better comply with international guidelines. In particular, services trade statistics in the BEA's U.S. International Transaction Accounts have been revised to incorporate new data sources as well as changes in classifications and other methodological improvements.

---

[13] WTO, *International Trade Statistics,* tables A8 and A9 (accessed November 17, 2014).

[14] In 2013, *Recent Trends* changed its format to cover three industries per year in depth, rotating on a four-year basis between professional services (education, healthcare, and legal or management consulting services); electronic services (audiovisual, computer, and telecommunication services); distribution services (logistics, retail, and transportation services (maritime transport)); and financial services (banking, insurance, and securities or leasing services). The 2014 report focused on electronic services.

[15] In this report, all multiyear growth rates are calculated as compound annual growth rates (average annual or annual growth rate). The annual growth rate is calculated as the geometric mean growth rate. For more information on the U.S. service economy, see USDOC, BEA, *Survey of Current Business,* October 2014.

[16] For more information on the BEA's data collection methods, see USDOC, BEA, *Survey of Current Business,* October 2014, 21.

These changes also include revisions to the historical data series on U.S. international transactions from the first quarter of 1999 through the fourth quarter of 2013.[17] All comparisons with previous years used in this report are based on the newly revised data. For this report, the Commission has supplemented the BEA data with information from other sources, including individual firms, trade associations, industry and academic journals and reports, international organizations, and other government agencies.

This introductory chapter examines the U.S. service sector, global trade in services, and U.S. trade in services. It reviews both cross-border trade in services from 2008 through 2013 and affiliate firms' sales of services from 2008 through 2012,[18] comparing the trade picture in recent years with earlier trends. Chapter 2 discusses trends affecting distribution services industries and examines their contribution to U.S. economic output, employment, labor productivity, and trade. Chapters 3, 4, and 5 focus on logistics services, maritime transport services, and retail services, respectively. These chapters provide an overview of market conditions, demand and supply factors, and recent trends in U.S. cross-border and affiliate trade for each industry. Chapter 6 summarizes the information presented and the views expressed at the eighth annual USITC services trade roundtable, hosted by the Commission in October 2014. Appendix A provides a snapshot of recent services research conducted by Commission staff.

The U.S. Services Sector

Services industries account for a large majority of U.S. production and employment. In 2013, U.S. services industries accounted for 78 percent (or $10.6 trillion) of total U.S. GDP and for 82 percent (or 87 million) of U.S. private sector full-time employees, compared to 22 percent and 18 percent, respectively, for the goods-producing sectors. Recent trends in the U.S. services sector have mirrored overall trends in the U.S. economy, with average annual growth rates of

---

[17] Notably, travel services trade numbers were revised in 2014 to reflect new electronic data collection procedures implemented by the U.S. Department of Homeland Security. These changes allowed more accurate accounting of passengers' destination countries and improved methods of estimating their travel-related spending (excluding online education services). For more information about how BEA has revised its data, see USDOC, BEA, "The Comprehensive Restructuring," March 2014, and USDOC, BEA, "Comprehensive Restructuring and Annual Revision," July 2014.

[18] "Affiliate firms" includes both firms outside the U.S. that are owned by U.S. companies and firms in the United States that are owned by foreign companies. Note that publication of the data on affiliate transactions lags publication of data on cross-border services trade by one year. Thus, while analyses of cross-border trade data compare performance in 2013 (the most recent year for which data are available) with trends from 2008 through 2012, analyses of affiliate transactions compare performance in 2012 with trends from 2008 through 2011. Note also that in 2009, the BEA changed its method of reporting affiliate trade data. These data now report "services supplied," a measure that better reflects services output than the prior measure, "sales of services." The change was retroactive for data from 2005 through 2008. For more information, see USDOC, BEA, *Survey of Current Business,* October 2009, 34–36.

services sector GDP, employment, and wages within 1 percent of the average annual growth rates registered for the United States as a whole from 2008 through 2013.[19]

Global Services Trade

The United States remains highly competitive in the global services market. As the world's top exporter of services, the United States accounted for $662.0 billion, or 14 percent, of global cross-border commercial services exports in 2013 (figure 1.1).[20] Other top single-country exporters included the United Kingdom and Germany, which accounted for about 6 percent each, or $292.7 and $286.2 billion respectively. Although most of the world's top 10 services exporters in 2013 were developed countries, China was the fifth-largest services exporter (after France), and India ranked sixth (up from seventh in 2012). Overall, the top 10 exporting countries together accounted for approximately 52 percent of global cross-border services exports in 2013.[21]

The United States was also the world's largest cross-border services importer in 2013, with $431.5 billion, or 10 percent, of global commercial services imports. China surpassed Germany to become the second-largest importer in 2013 with $329.4 billion (8 percent), compared to Germany's $316.8 billion (7 percent). India was the ninth-largest services importer (down from seventh in 2012). Overall, the top 10 importing countries accounted for 48 percent of global commercial services imports in 2013.[22]

The BEA publishes annual data on both U.S. cross-border trade and U.S. affiliate transactions in services, which together account for a substantial portion of the services provided through all four "modes of supply" specified in the General Agreement on Trade in Services (GATS) under the WTO (box 1.1). The BEA publishes these data by country and by industry, to the extent that

---

[19] USDOC, BEA, "Real Value Added by Industry," November 13, 2014; USDOC, BEA, Table 6.5D, "Full-Time Equivalent Employees by Industry," August 5, 2014; USDOC, BEA, Table 6.3D, "Wage and Salary Accruals," August 5, 2014. Value added is a measure of an industry's contribution to GDP; it is the difference between the value of an industry's gross output and the cost of its intermediate inputs. Full-time equivalent employees (FTEs) equal the number of employees on full-time schedules plus the number of employees on part-time schedules converted to a full-time basis. The number of FTEs in each industry is the product of the total number of employees and the ratio of average weekly hours per employee for all employees on full-time schedules.
[20] This discussion draws on WTO trade data to help compare U.S. trends with those of other countries. The term "commercial services," used by the WTO, is roughly equivalent to "private services" used by the BEA: both refer to services offered by the private, rather than the public sector. However, there are differences between the two values. These differences are the result of a lagged time period used for the WTO estimate and small differences in the activities captured by the two measures. USDOC, BEA representative, telephone interview by USITC staff, February 23, 2012.
[21] WTO, *International Trade Statistics 2013*, 2013, table A8.
[22] Ibid., table A9.

Figure 1.1: Global services: The United States led the world in cross-border exports and imports of services in 2013

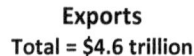

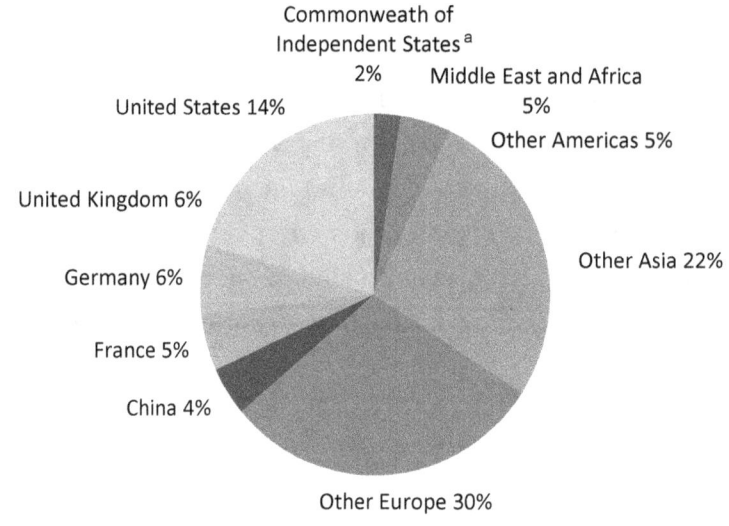

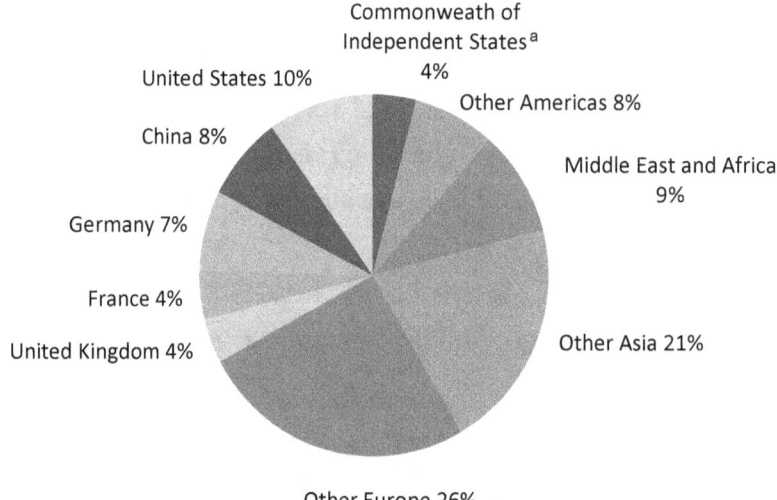

Source: WTO, *International Trade Statistics 2014*, 2014, tables A8 and A9. (See appendix table B.1.)
Notes: Excludes public sector transactions. Figures may not total to 100 percent due to rounding.
[a] The WTO includes the following countries under the Commonwealth of Independent States: Armenia, Azerbaijan, Belarus, Georgia, Kazakhstan, Kyrgyzstan, Moldova, Russia, Tajikistan, Turkmenistan, Ukraine, and Uzbekistan.

its surveys allow. The agency also publishes quarterly cross-border trade data in highly aggregated form.

According to the BEA, "cross-border trade" occurs when suppliers in one country sell services to consumers in another country, with people, information, or money crossing national boundaries in the process. Such transactions appear as exports and imports in a country's balance of payments. Firms also provide services to foreign consumers through affiliates established in host (i.e., foreign) countries; the income generated through "affiliate transactions" may appear as direct investment income in the balance of payments.[23]

The channel of delivery that service providers use is primarily determined by the nature of the service. For example, retail services are generally supplied through affiliates located close to consumers. In contrast, logistics and maritime transport services are predominantly traded across borders. Regardless, affiliate transactions (i.e., services provided by U.S. affiliates abroad) remain the principal means of providing services to foreign markets (box 1.2).

Box 1.1: Services trade "modes of supply" under the WTO's General Agreement on Trade in Services (GATS)

The GATS identifies four "modes of supply" for services trade—i.e., four ways that services can be traded:

Mode 1 is cross-border supply. In this mode, a service is supplied by an individual or firm in one country to an individual or firm in another (i.e., the service crosses national borders). An example would be a digital file of a final architectural design emailed to a foreign client. Mode 1 under the GATS does not directly compare to BEA's data for cross-border trade (see discussion below).

Mode 2 is consumption abroad. In this mode, an individual from one country travels to another country and consumes a service in that country. An example would be foreign nationals visiting the United States for medical care.

Mode 3 is commercial presence. In this mode, a firm based in one country establishes an affiliate in another country and supplies services from that locally established affiliate. An example would be a U.S.-based law firm providing legal services to citizens of a foreign country from its affiliated office located in that country.

Mode 4 is the temporary presence of natural persons. In this mode, an individual service supplier from one country travels to another country on a short-term basis to supply a service there—for instance, as a consultant, contract employee, or intracompany transferee at an affiliate in the host country.[a] An example would be U.S.-based engineers traveling to a foreign country to help local staff on a construction project.

---

[23] Income generated through affiliate transactions only appears as direct investment income in the balance of payments once it has been repatriated to the United States.

The BEA's data categories for services trade—i.e., cross-border trade and affiliate transactions—do not correspond exactly to the channels of service delivery described in the GATS.[b] The BEA notes that the GATS' mode 1 and mode 2 transactions, as well as some mode 4 transactions, generally are grouped together in the BEA's data on cross-border trade, while mode 3 transactions are included, with some exceptions, in the BEA's affiliate transactions data.

[a] USDOC, BEA, *Survey of Current Business*, October 2009, 40–43, tables 1 and 2.
[b] For more information on the four modes of supply under the GATS, see WTO, "Chapter 1: Basic Purpose and Concepts," n.d. (accessed April 7, 2009).

Box 1.2: The rise of affiliate transactions

Since 1986, when the U.S. Department of Commerce began collecting statistics on U.S. services trade, the relative importance of cross-border trade and affiliate transactions has shifted significantly. In each of the 10 years from 1986 through 1995, U.S. cross-border exports of services exceeded sales by U.S. majority-owned foreign affiliates of U.S. firms. Since 1996, however, sales by U.S. firms' foreign affiliates have exceeded exports of cross-border services. In 2012, services supplied by U.S. firms' affiliates abroad ($1.3 trillion) were almost double the value of U.S. cross-border exports of services ($662.9 billion). Similarly, services supplied to U.S. citizens by foreign-owned affiliates have exceeded cross-border services imports since 1989. In 2012, the value of services supplied to U.S. citizens by the U.S. affiliates of foreign companies ($801.9 billion) was nearly twice the value of U.S. services imports ($436.8 billion).[a]

The growing predominance of affiliate transactions largely reflects the global spread of service firms, facilitated by liberalization—the removal or lessening of barriers to trade—in investment and services. Liberalization first occurred in developed countries and has occurred more recently in a growing number of low- and middle-income countries.

[a] USDOC, BEA, *Survey of Current Business*, October 2014, 1–4.

Cross-border Trade, 2013

U.S. cross-border exports of private sector services totaled $662.9 billion in 2013, while U.S. imports totaled $436.8 billion, resulting in a $226.1 billion trade surplus (figure 1.2).[24] As in previous years, travel services and passenger fares are the categories with the largest share of U.S. services trade in 2013, together accounting for 32 percent of exports and 31 percent of imports.[25] Distribution services, by contrast, represented 7 percent of exports and 14 percent of imports (figure 1.3), resulting in a trade deficit of $13.6 billion in 2013.

---

[24] USDOC, BEA, *Survey of Current Business*, October 2014, 1–2.
[25] Ibid. Travel services are measured through foreign nationals' purchases of goods and services, such as food, lodging, recreation, local transportation, entertainment, and education- and health-related expenditures, while traveling abroad.

Figure 1.2: Majority-owned affiliate transactions continue to predominate as a means of trading services

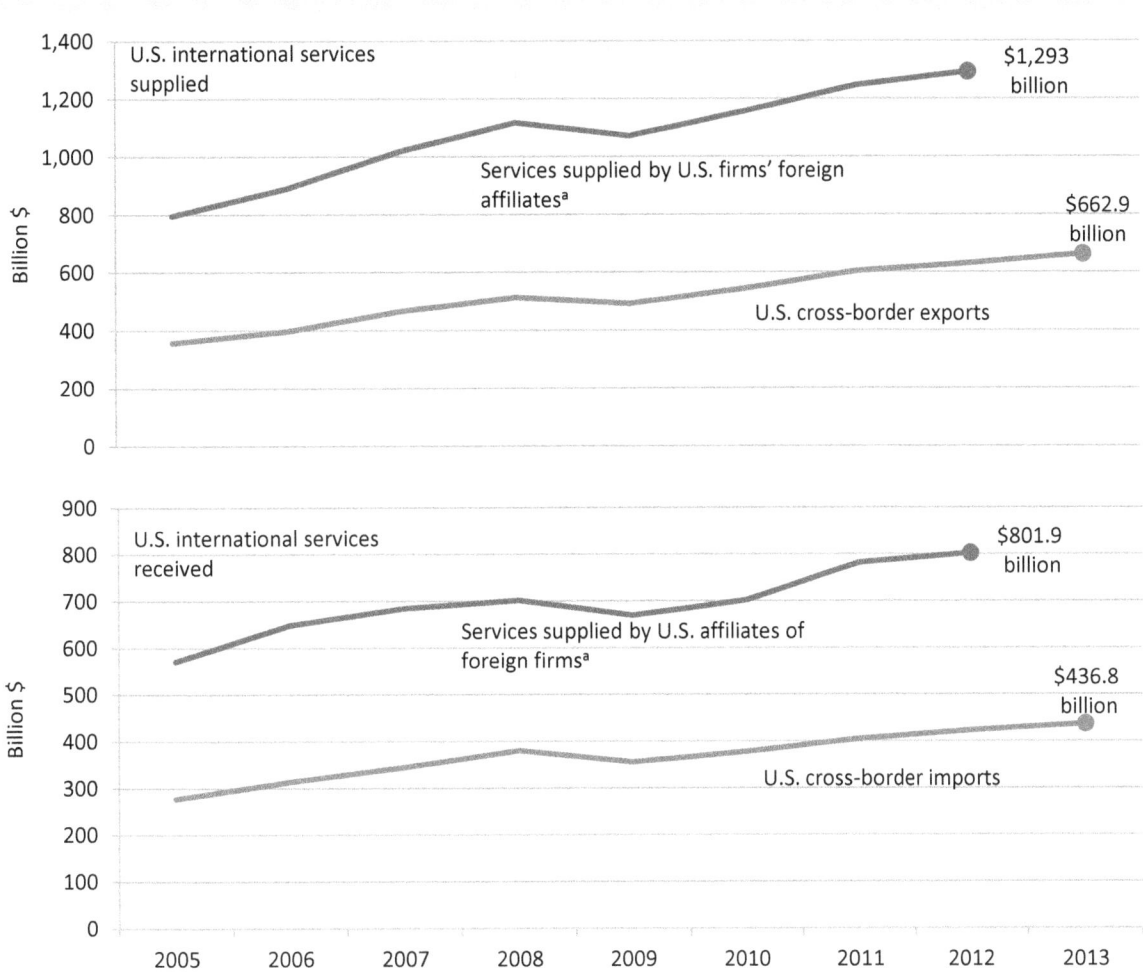

Source: USDOC, BEA, *Survey of Current Business,* October 2014, 1, 2, 19. (See appendix table B.2).
  [a] Data for affiliates are available only through 2012.

Figure 1.3: U.S. services: Travel and passenger fares accounted for the largest share of U.S. cross-border trade in 2013

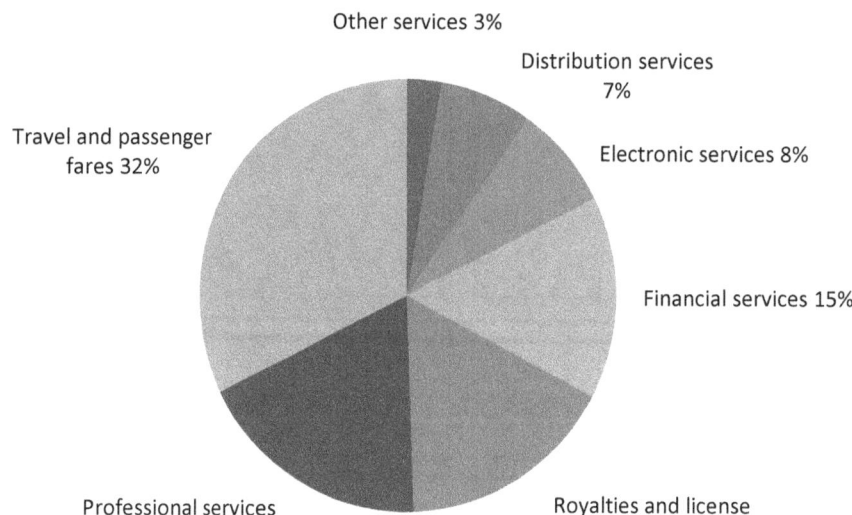

Exports
Total = $662.9 billion

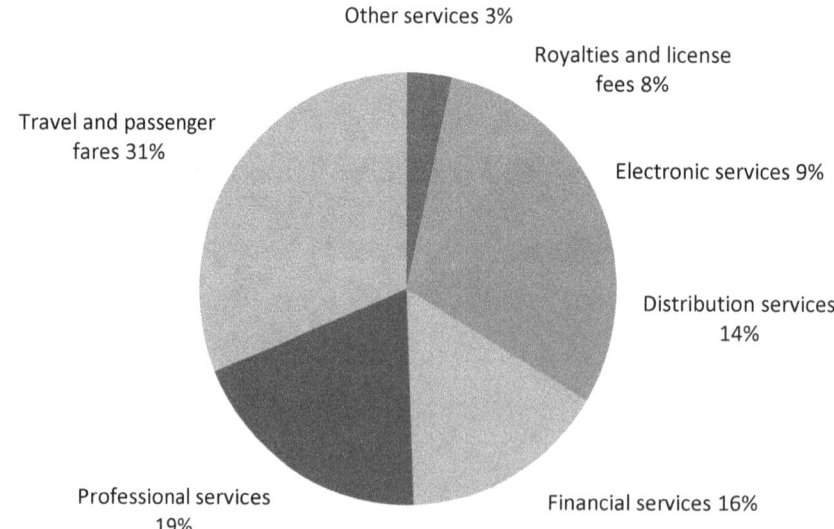

Imports
Total = $436.8 billion

Source: USDOC, BEA, *Survey of Current Business,* October 2014, 1–2 (See appendix table B.3).

In 2013, the value of U.S. cross-border services exports rose by 5 percent from 2012, which slightly exceeded the previous year's 4.5 percent increase.[26] Growth occurred in a number of service industries, led by finance and insurance (8 percent); travel (7 percent); professional services (5 percent); and royalties and licenses fees (3.9 percent).[27] Exports of distribution services also rose 2.2 percent, while electronic services increased a 1.6 percent. Other services exports decreased, driven by declines in exports in the construction sector and the sports and performing arts sector. At the same time, the value of U.S. services imports grew by 3 percent to $437.0 billion in 2013, a slightly slower pace than the previous year's 4.5 percent growth. Import growth was the highest for distribution services and professional services (6 percent each), followed by travel and other services (5 percent each) and electronic services (1 percent). Imports in the finance and insurance services and royalties and licenses services sectors both declined in 2013, driven by decreases in imports of both insurance services and other intellectual property services.[28]

As in previous years, the majority of U.S. service industries had cross-border trade surpluses in 2013. Travel achieved the largest surplus in 2013 ($78.1 billion), followed closely by royalties and licenses services ($77.0 billion), financial services ($65.0 billion), and professional services ($37.0 billion). Distribution services was the only sector with a cross-border trade deficit ($14.0 billion). However, several individual subsectors also recorded trade deficits, including insurance services ($34.0 billion), computer services ($11.0 billion), and research and development services ($2.1 billion).[29]

There were several reasons for those trade deficits. The deficit in distribution services[30] largely reflects the U.S. deficit in manufactured goods trade and the way in which U.S. imports of freight transportation services are measured.[31] The deficit in insurance services is principally the result of U.S. primary insurers' payments to European and Bermudian reinsurers in return

---

[26] Cross-border services trade, as reported in the current account, includes both private and public sector transactions. The latter principally reflect operations of the U.S. military and embassies abroad. However, because public sector transactions are not considered to reflect U.S. services industries' competitiveness and may introduce anomalies resulting from events such as international peacekeeping missions, this report will focus solely on private sector transactions, except as noted.

[27] USDOC, BEA, *Survey of Current Business,* October 2014, 2, table 1.

[28] Ibid.

[29] Ibid.

[30] BEA data on cross-border exports and imports of distribution services include data on air freight and airport services; sea freight and seaport services; and trade-related services. In 2013, the cross-border deficit in distribution services was driven by deficits in the airport, sea freight, and trade-related services categories.

[31] For example, Chinese shipments of manufactured goods to the United States typically exceed U.S. shipments of goods to China, and payments to Chinese or other foreign shippers for transporting U.S. merchandise imports are recorded by the BEA as U.S. imports of transportation services.

for their assuming a portion of large risks.[32] The deficit in computer services reflects U.S. firms offshoring many of these services to foreign providers, particularly those in India. For example, the United States imported $9.7 billion in computer services from India in 2013, a 2 percent increase over the previous year. Similarly, the deficit in research and development services also reflects firms' desire to reduce costs through outsourcing, as well as their need to gain flexibility and access a worldwide talent pool.[33]

Major U.S. trading partners in services have not significantly changed from 2012. A handful of developed countries continue to account for a substantial share of U.S. cross-border services trade. Canada, the United Kingdom, and Japan collectively received 25 percent of total U.S. cross-border services exports in 2013. Likewise, the United Kingdom (10 percent), Germany (7 percent), Canada and Japan (6 percent each), and Bermuda (5 percent) supplied the largest shares of U.S. services imports. In 2013, the European Union (EU) accounted for 30 percent of U.S. services exports and 35 percent of U.S. services imports.[34]

Cross-border Trade, 2014

Preliminary data for 2014 suggest that the majority of U.S. services exports and imports continued to grow that year. Annual services exports in 2014 exceeded those in 2013 by 3.4 percent, or $22.7 billion (table 1.1). Annual services imports in 2014 exceeded those in 2013 by 4.1 percent, or $17.7 billion. In addition, the U.S. services trade surplus grew by 2.2 percent, or $5.0 billion, in 2014.

Table 1.1: U.S. private services exports and imports to the world, by category, million dollars, 2013–14

Service industry	2013	2014	% change, 2013–14
Exports			
Travel	173,131	176,951	2.2
Charges for the use of intellectual property n.i.e.[a]	129,178	132,653	2.7
Financial services	84,066	88,418	5.2
Professional and management consulting services	55,758	59,312	6.4
Passenger fares	41,642	43,668	4.9
Technical, trade-related, and other business services[b]	37,637	36,633	-2.7
Research and development services	30,052	32,582	8.4
Air transport	23,880	24,070	0.8
Maintenance and repair services n.i.e.	16,295	18,710	14.8
Sea transport	17,175	18,107	5.4
Other	54,074	54,476	0.7
Total	662,888	685,580	3.4

---

[32] Reinsurance is a form of risk management whereby insurance companies buy insurance contracts from other insurers to protect themselves from unexpected large claims.

[33] PriceWaterhouseCoopers, *R&D Outsourcing in Hi-tech Industries*, September 2014, 3.

[34] USDOC, BEA, *Survey of Current Business,* October 2014, 3, table 2.

Service industry	2013	2014	% change, 2013–14
Imports			
Travel	104,677	111,714	6.7
Insurance services	50,454	49,315	-2.3
Charges for the use of intellectual property n.i.e.[a]	39,015	41,940	7.5
Professional and management consulting services	34,480	38,621	12.0
Sea transport	36,256	36,321	0.2
Passenger fares	32,029	34,890	8.9
Research and development services	32,142	33,776	5.1
Technical, trade-related and other business services[b]	26,088	24,212	-7.2
Computer services	23,643	24,208	2.4
Financial services	18,683	19,658	5.2
Other	39,324	39,842	1.3
Total	436,791	454,497	4.1

Source: USDOC, BEA, U.S. International Transaction Accounts Data, March 19, 2015, table 3.1.

Note: Data for 2014 are preliminary. n.i.e.=not included elsewhere.

[a] Charges for the use of intellectual property n.i.e. (formally classified as royalties and licenses fees) includes processes, computer software, trademarks and franchise fees, audiovisual and related products, and other intellectual property.

[b] Technical, trade-related, and other business includes construction, architectural and engineering services, waste treatment, operational leasing, trade-related, and other business services.

Affiliate Transactions, 2012

Services supplied by U.S.-owned foreign affiliates[35] grew by 3.7 percent to almost $1.3 trillion in 2012.[36] Distribution services—including wholesale trade, retail trade, and transportation and warehousing services—was the category that accounted for the largest share of affiliate transactions, with 31 percent of total services provided by U.S.-owned foreign affiliates (figure 1.4). Financial services ranked second, accounting for 20 percent of such sales. The largest foreign purchasers of services from U.S.-owned affiliates were the United Kingdom (UK) (15 percent), Canada (10 percent), and Japan and Ireland (6 percent each). The EU accounted for 43 percent of total services supplied by U.S.-owned affiliates in 2012.[37]

The value of services purchased from foreign-owned affiliates in the United States increased by 2.6 percent in 2012 to $801.9 billion as the U.S. economy continued to improve. This increase is 1 percent lower than the 3.7 percent average annual growth for the period 2008 through 2011.

---

[35] U.S.-owned foreign affiliates are affiliates owned by a U.S. parent company and located abroad; conversely, foreign-owned U.S. affiliates are affiliates located in the United States and owned by foreign parent companies.

[36] The main source for this section is the USDOC, BEA, *Survey of Current Business*, October 2014, 4–5, 19–23.

[37] USDOC, BEA, *Survey of Current Business,* October 2014, 19–23, tables 8–10.2.

Figure 1.4: U.S. services: Distribution services accounted for the largest share of U.S. affiliate transactions in 2012

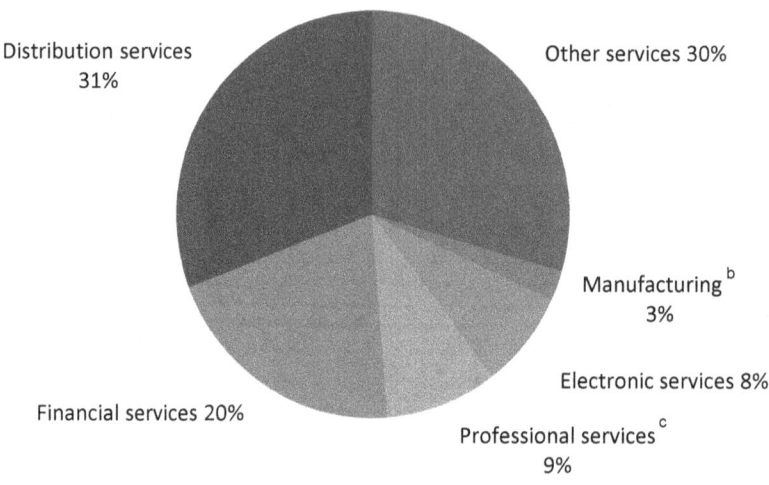

Services supplied by foreign affiliates of U.S. firms[a]
Total = $1,293.0 billion

Distribution services 31%

Other services 30%

Manufacturing [b] 3%

Electronic services 8%

Professional services [c] 9%

Financial services 20%

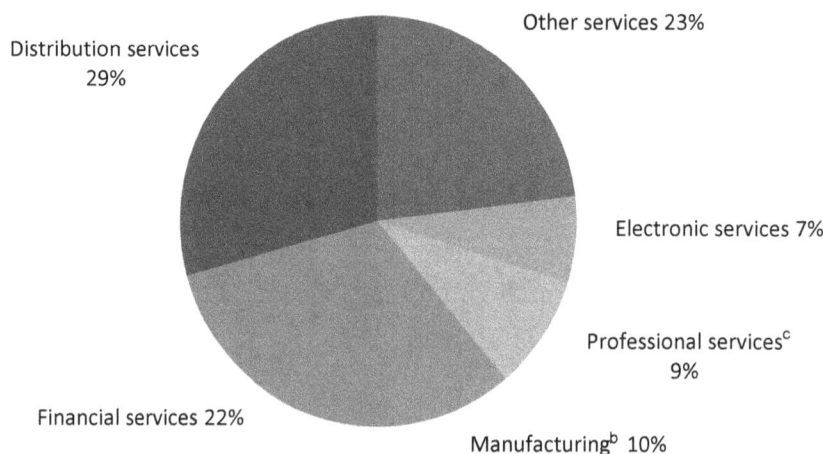

Purchases from U.S. affiliates of foreign firms[d]
Total = $801.9 billion

Distribution services 29%

Other services 23%

Electronic services 7%

Professional services[c] 9%

Manufacturing[b] 10%

Financial services 22%

Source: USDOC, BEA, *Survey of Current Business,* October 2014, 21, 23, tables 9.2 and 10.2. (See appendix table B.4).
[a] Services supplied by majority-owned foreign affiliates of U.S. parent firms.
[b] Includes ancillary services provided by goods manufacturers, such as computer hardware services.
[c] Data are underreported by the BEA to avoid disclosure of individual company information.
[d] Services supplied by majority-owned U.S. affiliates of foreign parent firms.

Distribution was again the category with the largest share in 2012, with 29 percent of purchases from foreign-owned affiliates in the United States, while financial services accounted for 22 percent and manufacturing services accounted for 10 percent. By country, German- and UK-owned firms supplied the largest share of such purchases in 2012 (15 percent each), followed by Japanese-owned firms (13 percent). French and Canadian affiliates rounded out the top five with 10 percent each. Overall, 53 percent of services purchased in the United States from foreign-owned affiliates in 2012 were from affiliates of EU-based parent firms.[38]

---

[38] Ibid.

Bibliography

PriceWaterhouseCoopers. *R&D Outsourcing in Hi-tech Industries: A Research Study.* PwC Research Insights. http://www.pwc.com/gx/en/pharma-life-sciences/high-tech-research-development-outsourcing.jhtml (accessed November 20, 2014).

U.S. Department of Commerce (USDOC). Bureau of Economic Analysis (BEA). Table 6.5D, "Full-Time Equivalent Employees by Industry." Interactive tables: Gross Domestic Product by Industry Accounts, November 17, 2014. http://www.bea.gov/iTable/iTable.cfm?ReqID=9&step=1#reqid=9&step=1&isuri=1&904=2008&903=197&906=q&905=2013&910=x&911=0.

———. "Comprehensive Restructuring and Annual Revision," July 2014. http://www.bea.gov/scb/pdf/2014/07%20July/0714_annual_international_transactions_accounts.pdf.

———. "The Comprehensive Restructuring of International Economic Accounts," March 2014. http://www.bea.gov/scb/pdf/2014/03%20March/0314_restructuring_the_international_economic_accounts.pdf.

———. "Real Value Added by Industry." Interactive tables: Gross Domestic Product by Industry Accounts, November 13, 2014. http://www.bea.gov/iTable/iTable.cfm?ReqID=51&step=1#reqid=51&step=2&isuri=1.

———. *Survey of Current Business* 89, no. 10 (October 2009).

———. *Survey of Current Business* 94, no. 10 (October 2014).

———. Table 6.3D: "Wage and Salary Accruals per Full Time Equivalent Employee by Industry." Interactive tables: National and Product Accounts, August 5, 2014. http://www.bea.gov/iTable/iTable.cfm?ReqID=9&step=1#reqid=9&step=3&isuri=1&904=2008&903=197&906=q&905=2013&910=x&911=0.

World Trade Organization (WTO). *International Trade Statistics 2014*, n.d. Table A8, "World Exports of Commercial Services by Region and Selected Economy, 2003–2013." http://www.wto.org/english/res_e/statis_e/its2014_e/its14_appendix_e.htm (accessed November 17, 2014).

———. *International Trade Statistics 2014*, n.d. Table A9, "World Imports of Commercial Services by Region and Selected Economy, 2003–2013." http://www.wto.org/english/res_e/statis_e/its2014_e/its14_appendix_e.htm (accessed November 17, 2014).

Chapter 2
Distribution Services

Overview

Distribution services[39] refer to the wide range of activities that facilitate the movement of goods throughout the supply chain—from producer to end consumer. While wholesale and retail services firms form the core of the distribution services industry, logistics and transportation services companies provide the vital link between manufacturer, wholesaler, retailer, and final customer. The distribution services industry also includes several types of firms that ease the conveyance of intermediate and final goods through complex, and increasingly global, distribution networks. These intermediaries include, for instance, freight forwarders (which typically consolidate cargo for delivery by air or ocean freight) and third-party logistics providers (which coordinate and manage the movement of goods through each node of the supply chain).[40]

An efficient distribution services sector enables the global trading system and improves overall economic welfare. By contrast, inefficient distribution services can lead to misallocation of resources and a rise in economic costs.[41] Generally, lower distribution services costs are associated with integration of markets within an economy and with the integration of those domestic markets with the rest of the world. These linkages support economic development and contribute to income growth. Efficient distribution firms also enable consumers around the

---

[39] Although the WTO defines "distribution services" to include only retail and wholesale services, this report uses a broader definition that includes the activities of logistics and transportation services firms. WTO, "Distribution Services: Background Note by the Secretariat," October 29, 2010, 3. Wholesale services was not given a separate chapter in this report. However, since BEA trade data on wholesale activity are available, those numbers will be included in the broader distribution services trade discussion. According to BEA, wholesale trade consists of (1) merchant wholesalers that sell goods on their own account, and (2) business-to-business (B2B) electronic markets, agents, and brokers that arrange transactions for others, usually for a commission or fee. USDOC, BEA, *Guide to Industry Classifications for International Surveys,* December 2007, 30.

[40] WTO, "Distribution Services: Background Note by the Secretariat," October 29, 2010, 3; SelectUSA, "The Logistics and Transportation Industry," n.d. (accessed November 18, 2014).

[41] For example, if distribution services are unreliable and infrequent, or if a country lacks third-party logistics providers who efficiently handle goods shipments, firms are likely to maintain higher inventory holdings—at every stage of the supply chain. The costs of financing large inventories can be significant, especially in countries with high real interest rates. Mattoo, Stern, and Zanini, *A Handbook of International Trade in Services,* 2007, 356–59; WTO, "Services: Sector by Sector: Distribution Services," n.d. (accessed October 7, 2014).

world to benefit more fully from the liberalization of trade restrictions, making it possible for them to access a diverse array of products at lower prices.[42]

Ultimately, trade in distribution services is shaped by spending on consumer goods. However, the industry is also evolving rapidly in response to shifting global supply chains, advances in digital technology, and increasing cost competition across all factors of production and distribution.[43]

Consumer Merchandise Demand Drives Distribution Services

The demand for distribution services, and hence the health of the distribution services industry, depends heavily on consumer merchandise demand. Adverse economic conditions thus undermine the revenues of distribution services firms. For instance, the global recession of 2008–09 had a profound negative impact on almost all segments of the distribution services industry, as declining disposable incomes and low confidence in global financial markets led consumers to cut back sharply on purchases of a broad range of goods and services.[44] This steep decline in consumer spending first affected the retail services industry—including both brick-and-mortar stores and online retailers—with the cutbacks soon reverberating backward up the supply chain. Weak consumer spending lowered retailers' purchases from wholesalers, in turn reducing the wholesalers' need for warehousing and storage services and freight transportation services.[45] Conversely, improving economic conditions in the United States had a positive effect on U.S. distribution services firms in 2010–13. Economic recovery and a resulting rise in consumer spending bolstered not only the performance of U.S. manufacturing, wholesale, and retail sectors, but also that of complementary industries like warehousing, long-distance trucking, and rail transport services.[46]

---

[42] Because the costs associated with distribution make up a significant portion of the retail price of most goods—typically between 10 and 50 percent—the distribution sector plays a major role in price formation, with more efficient systems helping to lower prices. Pilat, "Regulation and Performance," 1997, 3.

[43] Shipping costs are often more important obstacles to entry into export markets than policy barriers. Mattoo, Stern, and Zanini, *A Handbook of International Trade in Services*, 2007, 356–59.

[44] This report uses time frames based on data availability—depending on the sources used, industry-level analyses may cover slightly different years. However, presentation of U.S. services trade data will largely remain consistent across the report.

[45] WTO, "Distribution Services: Background Note by the Secretariat," October 29, 2010, 12. Transportation services, along with passenger fares, experienced the largest declines in imports and exports of any services industry in 2009 during the height of the recession. USDOC, BEA, *Survey of Current Business*, October 2010, 19.

[46] Stynes, "Union Pacific Profit Rises 19%," October 23, 2014; Biery, "U.S. Trucking Companies Deliver Sales, Profit Gains," February 20, 2014; Leubsdorf, "U.S. Economic Growth Could Get Boost," December 2014.

Distribution Services Firms Have Grown More "Adaptive" in Response to Changes in Demand and New Technology

In recent years, supply chains have shifted to reflect new manufacturing trends on the one hand, and new ways to market and deliver finished goods to consumers on the other. The rapid rise of digital technologies, including Internet sales platforms and online ordering, have enabled many sellers to move away from traditional storefronts in the United States and to reach new customers in foreign markets—and has inevitably affected distribution services providers (figure 2.1).[47] For many manufacturers, of both intermediate and final goods as demand from new markets continues to grow, "near- shoring"[48] is increasingly replacing production processes that had grown geographically fragmented and/or too costly to maintain.[49] Consequently, these manufacturers are requiring distribution services firms to reconfigure transport routes to better serve their regional production centers and accommodate shorter time frames. With the development of advanced manufacturing techniques, such as 3-D printing,[50] opportunities for manufacturers to further compress the distribution services supply chain grows. For instance, using 3-D printing technology, manufacturers may be able to more easily produce their own customized parts rather than rely on specialized upstream suppliers,[51] potentially reducing the need for wholesaling and warehousing services.[52]

---

[47] USITC, *Digital Trade, Part 1*, July 2013, table F-1.

[48] Near-shoring (also called near-sourcing or reshoring) is the practice of moving production processes closer to firms' target markets, generally in order to cut transportation costs and increase supply chain flexibility. By contrast, "offshoring" occurs when firms move production overseas regardless of the location of target markets. Cagliano, De Marco, and Rafele, "The Impact of Near Sourcing," 2013.

[49] Near-shoring has been seen in a wide range of industries, including in the manufacture of computers and electronics, household appliances, home furniture, and apparel. Although difficult to track with precise statistics across countries, several industry surveys have documented the growing importance of near-shoring as a means of reducing labor and/or fuel costs, among others. *Economist*, "Reshoring Manufacturing: Coming Home," January 19, 2013.

[50] 3-D printing refers to a process in which an individual machine, through the successive layering of material, creates a three-dimensional product. *Economist*, "Reshoring Manufacturing: Coming Home," January 19, 2013. For a fuller discussion, see chapter 3, "Logistics Services."

[51] Cohen, Sargent, and Somers, "3D Printing Takes Shape," January 2014.

[52] Manners-Bell and Lyon, "The Implications of 3D Printing," January 23, 2014.

Figure 2.1: Distribution services supply chain: Technology has increasingly enabled manufacturers to bypass traditional wholesalers and retailers

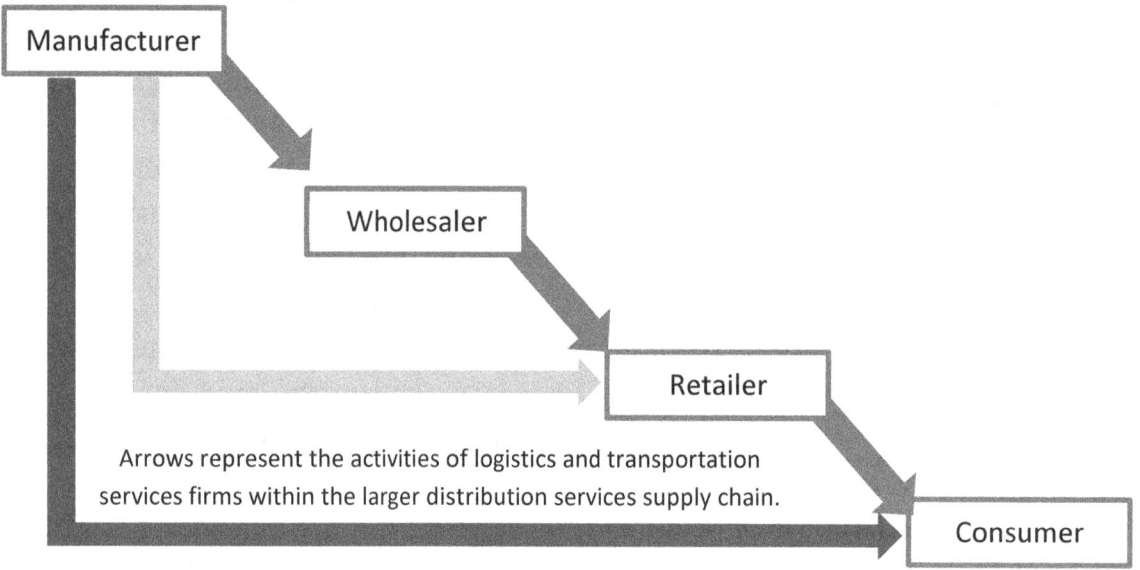

Source: Compiled by USITC.

The growing use of Internet technologies to buy goods (e-commerce) has also required better coordination among retail, logistics, and transportation services firms. For example, online retailers have invested heavily in improving order-fulfillment infrastructure, as demand for two-day and even same-day shipping for certain products has risen.[53] Moreover, some distribution services firms with established e-commerce platforms are serving as "virtual" marketplaces that coordinate independent sellers and facilitate marketing and payment services.[54]

Companies with a physical retailing presence are overcoming space limitations by taking advantage of e-commerce to sell a wider range of products. However, as e-commerce eliminates the "physical" barriers to retail trade, it also opens domestic retailers to increased competition from foreign businesses that might otherwise have difficulty entering new markets.[55]

---

[53] Morgan Stanley Research, "eCommerce Disruption: A Global Theme," January 6, 2013, 5.

[54] The online retailer Amazon is increasingly taking on the features of a third-party logistics company by coordinating independent sellers on its website in addition to its core business as a product vendor. Lieb and Lieb, "Is Amazon a 3PL?" 2014. Other online-only businesses (e.g., eBay) are able to reach more potential customers without the expense or geographical limitations of brick-and-mortar stores, and also allow existing retailers to test new markets with fewer risks. Deloitte, "From Bricks to Clicks: Generating Global Growth," 2014, 1.

[55] MacKenzie, Meyer, and Noble, "How Retailers Can Keep Up with Consumers," October 2013.

Distribution Services Providers Compete on Costs

The distribution services industry generally has high barriers to entry. Most segments of the industry must nonetheless confront intense competition, both between companies in the same industry segment (internal competition) and between industry segments (external competition). The retail industry, for example, is noted for its strong competition between specialty retailers, department stores, discount retailers, mail-order catalogs, direct-to-consumer companies, and online retailers. However, retailers also face competition external to the industry when, for example, manufacturers ship goods directly to consumers, bypassing retailers (and wholesalers) entirely. Some brands, in apparel and electronics, are building their own brick-and-mortar retailing arms.[56]

The need to expand to new markets is also driving retailers to innovate. Some big-box retailers (e.g., Walmart and Target) have developed smaller-format stores with different product mixes for urban areas where they were previously absent. Other retailers, particularly in the grocery sector, are increasingly marketing in-house brands to customers, allowing them to capture more revenue by vertically integrating parts of their supply chain.[57]

In other distribution services industries, increasing competition has limited the ability of companies to raise (or even maintain) prices. Consequently, many have focused instead on cutting internal costs and making their operations more efficient in an effort to remain profitable. In the shipping industry, for instance, the introduction of increasingly larger ships has increased economies of scale in the movement of cargo,[58] and concerns about efficiency are motivating logistics firms to improve their data management capabilities.[59] To illustrate, some logistics companies are integrating data programs with GPS systems. Using these, they can sort through large amounts of information to calculate optimal transportation routes and streamline inventory management.[60]

---

[56] Miller and Clifford, "E-Commerce Companies Bypass the Middlemen," March 31, 2013; WTO, "Distribution Services: Background Note by the Secretariat," October 29, 2010, 13.

[57] Malouff, "Walmart's 6 DC Stores," April 26, 2012; Miller and Clifford, "E-Commerce Companies Bypass the Middlemen," March 31, 2013; WTO, "Distribution Services: Background Note by the Secretariat," October 29, 2010, 13.

[58] A.P. Moller-Maersk A/S, *Annual Report 2013,* 2013, 27.

[59] Fuel costs are also a concern for transportation services firms. If fuel prices continue to fall in the long term, this is likely to lower the operating costs of logistics, maritime, and other transportation services providers.

[60] Marle, "A New Era for Supply Chains," September 16, 2014.

U.S. Trade in Distribution Services

Distribution services represented a small but material share of U.S. services trade in 2013, accounting for 7 percent of total U.S. cross-border services exports and 14 percent of U.S. cross-border services imports.[61] In that year, U.S. cross-border exports of distribution services totaled $46.6 billion, whereas imports totaled $60.2 billion, resulting in a trade deficit of $13.6 billion.[62]

Logistics services (including air freight and airport services) represented 51 percent ($23.9 billion) of total U.S. distribution services exports and 30 percent ($18.2 billion) of imports in 2013, producing a small trade surplus of nearly $6.0 billion (figure 2.2). Maritime transport services (including both maritime freight and port services) accounted for 36.8 percent ($17.2 billion) of distribution services' exports and 60 percent ($36.3 billion) of imports, for a much larger trade deficit of $19.1 billion. In 2013, the top three markets for U.S. exports of logistics services were the United Kingdom (17 percent), Germany (7 percent), and Japan (6 percent), while the leading markets for U.S. exports of maritime transport services were Japan (13 percent), Taiwan (9 percent), and Germany (8 percent).[63]

Affiliate transactions (GATS mode 3; see box 1.1) accounted for the vast majority of U.S. trade in distribution services in 2012.[64] During that year, U.S.-owned foreign affiliates (i.e., overseas affiliates of U.S. companies) supplied $399.0 billion of such services, representing the largest category of services supplied by U.S.-owned foreign affiliates (31 percent share). Within distribution services, wholesale trade accounted for the majority of services supplied by U.S. affiliates abroad (60 percent) (figure 2.3). Retail trade also accounted for a significant share (25 percent) of sales by U.S.-owned foreign affiliates, reaching $101 million in 2012.[65] By

---

[61] USDOC, BEA, *Survey of Current Business*, October 2014, table 1, "U.S. Trade in Services, 2003–13," 1–2. For the purposes of the cross-border trade discussion, data on distribution services encompass air transport services (e.g., air freight and port services); maritime transport services (e.g., maritime freight and port services); other modes of transport (e.g., road and rail transport services); and trade-related services (e.g., auction services, business-to-business transaction fees, Internet-based commercial exchanges, and commissions paid to independent sales agents). BEA does not collect cross-border data on retail services.

[62] USDOC, BEA, *Survey of Current Business,* October 2014, table 1, "U.S. Trade in Services, 2003–13," 1–2.

[63] USDOC, BEA, *Survey of Current Business,* October 2014, table 13-2.

[64] USDOC, BEA, *Survey of Current Business,* October 2014, table 1. For the purposes of the discussion on affiliate transactions in distribution services, data include those pertaining to wholesale and retail trade, as well as air transportation services, water transportation services, rail transportation services, truck transportation services, and support activities for transportation.

[65] USDOC, BEA, *Survey of Current Business,* October 2014, table 9.2.

Figure 2.2: U.S. distribution services: Logistics services led cross-border exports and maritime transport led cross-border imports of distribution services in 2013

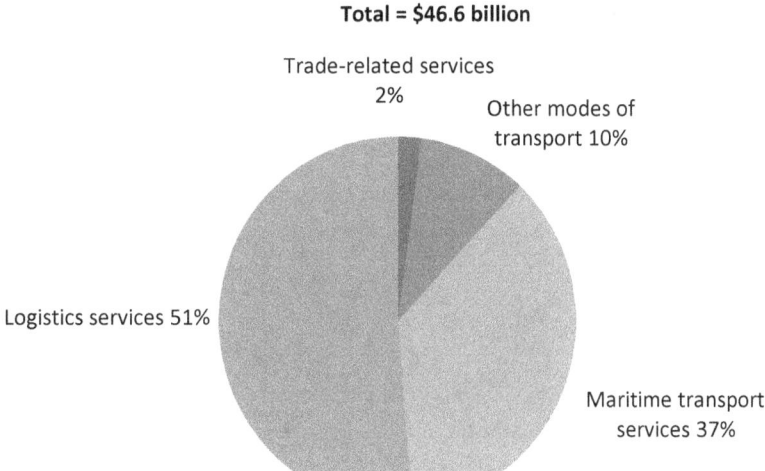

Exports
Total = $46.6 billion

Trade-related services 2%

Other modes of transport 10%

Logistics services 51%

Maritime transport services 37%

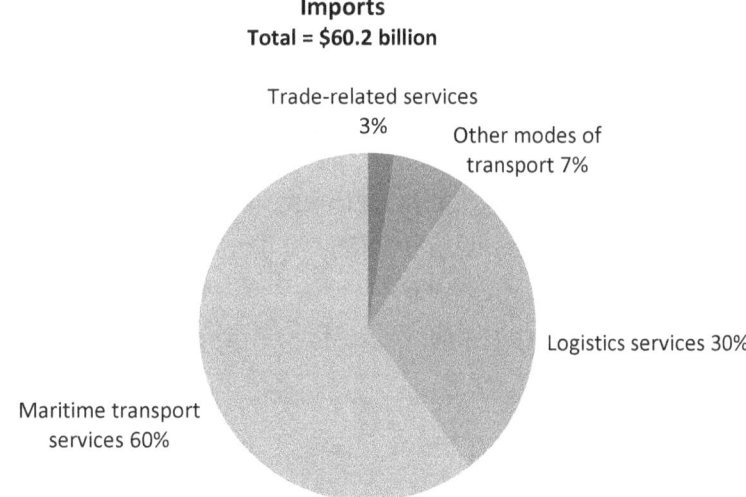

Imports
Total = $60.2 billion

Trade-related services 3%

Other modes of transport 7%

Logistics services 30%

Maritime transport services 60%

Source: USDOC, BEA, *Survey of Current Business,* October 2014, 1, 2, table 1. (See appendix table B.5.)
Note: Excludes public-sector transactions.

Figure 2.3: Wholesale trade was the largest category of distribution services supplied by U.S. affiliates abroad in 2012

Source: USDOC, BEA, *Survey of Current Business*, October 2014, 21, 23, tables 9.2 and 10.2. (See appendix table B.6.)
Notes: Trade data exclude public sector transactions. Data on logistics services include air transportation, rail transportation, truck transportation, and support activities for transportation but do not include "other" transportation and warehousing services. Totals for foreign-owned U.S. affiliates of logistics services firms are underreported due to suppression of data by the BEA to safeguard confidentiality.

comparison, logistics and maritime transport services accounted for only 5 percent and 2 percent, respectively, of total sales by U.S. affiliates abroad.

The value of distribution services purchased from foreign-owned U.S. affiliates (i.e., affiliates of foreign firms located in the United States) was $235.0 billion in 2012. Wholesale trade accounted for the largest share (60 percent) of purchases from foreign-owned U.S. affiliates, totaling $142.0 billion, while retail trade accounted for 19 percent of such purchases.[66]

---

[66] Ibid. Purchases from foreign-owned U.S. affiliates are underreported due to the BEA's suppression of data in the air and rail transportation categories to avoid disclosing confidential and/or company-specific information.

GDP, Employment, Labor Productivity, and Salaries

In 2013, the contribution of U.S. private sector distribution services to U.S. private sector GDP (including goods and services) was $2.3 trillion, accounting for nearly 17 percent of total U.S. private sector GDP (table 2.1).[67] Wholesale and retail trade each represented about 40 percent of distribution services' contribution to U.S. private sector GDP in the year, followed by logistics services (18 percent), and maritime transport services (1 percent). Distribution services grew by 1.7 percent, slightly slower than the GDP growth of 2.2 percent for the U.S. private sector as a whole in 2013 (table 2.2).

Table 2.1: United States: GDP, FTEs, wage and salary accruals, and labor productivity, by goods and services industry, 2008–13

	2008	2012	2013	CAGR 2008–12	% change 2012–13
GDP (billion $)					
Private sector	12,793	13,190	13,481	0.8	2.2
Goods	2,908	2,857	2,922	-0.4	2.3
Manufacturing	1,869	1,837	1,863	-0.4	1.4
Nonmanufacturing	1,038	1,020	1,059	-0.4	3.9
Services	9,874	10,329	10,554	1.1	2.2
Distribution services	2,244	2,213	2,251	-0.3	1.7
Financial services	1,023	1,194	1,248	4.0	4.5
Professional services	2,384	2,446	2,488	0.6	1.7
Electronic services	719	787	815	2.3	3.6
Other services	3,517	3,692	3,758	1.2	1.8
FTEs (thousands)					
Private sector	108,029	104,358	106,909	-0.9	2.4
Goods	22,122	19,121	19,514	-3.6	2.1
Manufacturing	13,142	11,662	11,749	-2.9	0.7
Nonmanufacturing	8,980	7,459	7,765	-4.5	4.1
Services	85,907	85,237	87,395	-0.2	2.5
Distribution services	23,598	22,560	22,882	-1.1	1.4
Financial services	6,425	6,162	6,225	-1.0	1.0
Professional services	25,542	26,649	27,671	1.1	3.8
Electronic services	3,317	3,291	3,399	-0.2	3.3
Other services	27,025	26,575	27,218	-0.4	2.4
Wages and salary accruals ($ per FTE)					
Private sector	51,239	56,167	56,554	2.3	0.7
Goods	54,327	60,516	61,252	2.7	1.2
Manufacturing	56,352	62,974	63,628	2.8	1.0
Nonmanufacturing	51,362	56,672	57,658	2.5	1.7
Services	48,863	53,793	54,124	2.4	0.6

---

[67] USDOC, BEA, "Real Value Added by Industry," 2014. By contrast, financial services accounted for 9 percent of total U.S. private sector GDP in 2013, while professional services accounted for 18 percent; electronic services, 6 percent; and other services (including real estate), 28 percent.

	2008	2012	2013	CAGR 2008–12	% change 2012–13
Distribution services	42,249	46,154	46,671	2.2	1.1
Financial services	84,678	91,485	92,115	2.0	0.7
Professional services	56,994	62,384	62,107	2.3	-0.4
Electronic services	81,866	95,987	96,188	4.1	0.2
Other services	34,379	37,697	38,333	2.3	1.7
Labor productivity ($ per FTE)					
Private sector	118,424	126,387	126,101	1.6	-0.2
Goods	131,430	149,401	149,739	3.3	0.2
Manufacturing	142,223	157,503	158,533	2.6	0.7
Nonmanufacturing	115,635	136,734	136,433	4.3	-0.2
Services	114,941	121,181	120,762	1.3	-0.3
Distribution services	95,080	98,090	98,370	0.8	0.3
Financial services	159,191	193,833	200,466	5.0	3.4
Professional services	93,336	91,793	89,899	-0.4	-2.1
Electronic services	216,611	239,137	239,806	2.5	0.3
Other services	130,128	138,943	138,063	1.7	-0.6

Source: USDOC, BEA, "Full-Time Equivalent Employees by Industry," 2014.
Note: CAGR or compound annual growth rate.

Table 2.2: United States: GDP, FTEs, wage and salary accruals, and labor productivity, by services industry, 2008–13

	2008	2012	2013	CAGR 2008–12	% change 2012–13
GDP (billion $)					
Wholesale trade	943.4	893.6	907.6	-1.3	1.6
Retail trade	866.4	881.8	902.8	0.4	2.4
Logistics services	401.7	404.9	408.1	0.2	0.8
Maritime transport services	13.9	17.1	18.7	5.3	9.4
Other distribution services	18	16	14	-4.1	-11.6
FTEs (thousands)					
Wholesale trade	5,796	5,472	5,554	-1.4	1.5
Retail trade	13,481	12,886	13,078	-1.1	1.5
Logistics services	4,218	4,099	4,146	-0.7	1.1
Maritime transport services	64	62	63	-0.8	1.6
Other distribution services	39	41	41	1.3	0.0
Wages and salary accruals ($ per FTE)					
Wholesale trade	64,920	71,956	72,362	2.6	0.6
Retail trade	30,715	33,196	33,522	2.0	1.0
Logistics services	46,949	50,964	52,391	2.1	2.8
Maritime transport services	75,498	83,032	84,372	2.4	1.6
Other distribution services	104,282	107,077	112,100	0.7	4.7
Labor productivity ($ per FTE)					
Wholesale trade	162,767	163,304	163,414	0.1	0.1
Retail trade	64,268	68,431	69,032	1.6	0.9
Logistics services	95,235	98,780	98,432	0.9	0.4
Maritime transport services	217,188	275,806	296,825	6.2	7.6
Other distribution services	469,231	378,049	334,146	-5.3	-11.6

Sources: USDOC, BEA, "Full-Time Equivalent Employees by Industry," 2014.
Note: CAGR or compound annual growth rate.

Among the distribution services industries, the GDP of maritime transport services grew the fastest in 2013 at 9.4 percent, followed by retail trade (2.4 percent), wholesale trade (1.6 percent), and logistics services (1 percent).

The distribution services sector was one of the most important contributors to U.S. private sector employment in 2013. Overall, the sector employed 23 million full-time equivalent (FTE) employees, or more than 20 percent of the total U.S. private sector workforce—a share that has remained stable since 2008.[68] In 2013, retail services employed nearly 13 million people, accounting for 57 percent of total distribution services employment, followed by wholesale services (24 percent) and logistics services (18 percent). In step with employment trends in the broader U.S. economy, the number of FTEs in the distribution services sector fell by an average of about 1 percent each year during 2008–12, resulting in the loss of slightly more than 1 million FTEs total. In 2013, however, employment in the sector partially recovered, growing by more than 1 percent in the aggregate (and in each of the distribution services industries). Overall, though, total employment in the sector remained slightly lower in 2013 than in 2008.[69]

Although employment in distribution services declined during 2008–13, labor productivity— measured as output in dollars per FTE—grew at a steady, but modest, pace. During the period, labor productivity in distribution services grew at an annual rate of only 1 percent, as a slight increase in sector output over the period exceeded the small decrease in employment.[70] In 2013, average output per worker in the distribution services sector was $98,370, substantially lower than in electronic services ($239,806) and financial services ($200,466) but surpassing labor productivity in professional services ($89,899). By contrast, output per worker in the manufacturing sector was $158,533 in 2013. Within the distribution services sector, output per worker varied widely by industry, ranging from $69,032 in the labor-intensive retail services industry to $296,825 in the capital-intensive maritime transport services industry.[71]

Workers in the distribution services sector earned, on average, $46,671 in 2013, lower than the private sector average of $56,554 and significantly trailing average wages in electronic services

---

[68] USDOC, BEA, "Full-Time Equivalent Employees by Industry," 2014.

[69] The number of FTEs in 2008 was estimated to be 23,598,000 compared to 22,882,000 in 2013, for a loss of roughly 716,000 FTEs.

[70] USDOC, BEA, "Full-Time Equivalent Employees by Industry," 2014; USDOC, BEA, "Real Value Added by Industry," 2014.

[71] Average output per worker in the professional services sector is generally lower, since healthcare and social assistance FTEs make up 58 percent of this category. These sectors are both very labor intensive and subject to higher administrative costs as a result of a heavier regulatory burden. Moreover, output per worker in the maritime transport services industry is likely higher as a result of investments in new technologies and infrastructure to handle cargo more efficiently. U.S. port services firms are also investing in automation in an attempt to control labor costs in order to remain competitive. Kocher, "The Downside of Healthcare Jobs Growth," September 23, 2013; Scheyder, "Analysis: U.S. Ports' Drive to Control Costs," January 17, 2013.

($96,188), financial services ($92,115), and professional services ($62,107).[72] Like labor productivity, average annual wages in the distribution services sector covered a wide range— from $33,522 in retail services to $84,372 in maritime transport services. During 2008–12, wages in distribution services grew at an annual rate of roughly 2.2 percent, on par with the other sectors of the economy, except for electronic services, where wages grew by 4 percent. In 2013, however, wage growth in distribution services slowed to 1.1 percent, which was still faster than in other important services industries, including financial services (0.7 percent), electronic services (0.2 percent), and professional services (-0.4 percent).

---

[72] USDOC, BEA, "Wage and Salary Accruals by Industry," 2014.

Bibliography

A.P. Moller-Maersk A/S. *Annual Report 2013,* 2013.
http://files.shareholder.com/downloads/ABEA-
3GG91Y/3816066656x0x731491/FB0012EF-15F0-4FDA-80E0-
D9A1B00B698E/Annual_Report_2013.pdf.

Biery, Mary Ellen. "U.S. Trucking Companies Deliver Sales, Profit Gains." *Forbes,* February
20, 2014. http://www.forbes.com/sites/sageworks/2014/02/20/sales-profit-trends-
trucking-companies/.

Cagliano, Anna Corinna, Alberto De Marco, and Carlo Rafele. "The Impact of Near Sourcing on
Global Dynamic Supply Chains: A Case Study." In *Dynamics in Logistics: Proceedings of
Third International Conference, LDIC 2012 Bremen, Germany, February /March 2012,*
edited by H-J. Kreowski, B. Scholz-Reiter, and K-D. Thoben, 489–98. Springer Verlag,
2013.
http://www.researchgate.net/publication/258506568_The_Impact_of_Near_Sourcing_
on_Global_Dynamic_Supply_Chains_A_Case_Study.

Cohen, David, Matthew Sargent, and Ken Somers. "3D Printing Takes Shape." *McKinsey
Quarterly,* January 2014. http://www.mckinsey.com/insights/manufacturing/3-
d_printing_takes_shape.

Corridore, Jim. "Transportation: Commercial." S&P Capital IQ Industry Surveys,
September 2014.

Deloitte. "From Bricks to Clicks: Generating Global Growth through eCommerce Expansion,"
2014. http://www2.deloitte.com/content/dam/Deloitte/za/Documents/consumer-
business/za_generating_growth_through_ecommerce_24112014.pdf.

Economist. "Reshoring Manufacturing: Coming Home," January 19, 2013.
http://www.economist.com/news/special-report/21569570-growing-number-american-
companies-are-moving-their-manufacturing-back-united.

Kocher, Robert. "The Downside of Healthcare Jobs Growth." *Harvard Business Review,*
September 23, 2013. https://hbr.org/2013/09/the-downside-of-health-care-job-
growth/.

Leubsdorf, Ben. "U.S. Economic Growth Could Get Boost from Services Spending." *Wall Street
Journal,* December 10, 2014. http://blogs.wsj.com/economics/2014/12/10/u-s-
economic-growth-could-get-boost-from-services-spending/.

Lieb, Robert, and Kristin Lieb. "Is Amazon a 3PL?" *Supplychain Quarterly: Logistics,* Quarter 3,
2014. http://www.supplychainquarterly.com/topics/Logistics/20141027-is-amazon-a-
3pl/.

MacKenzie, Ian, Chris Meyer, and Steve Noble. "How Retailers Can Keep Up with Consumers." *McKinsey Quarterly,* October 2013. http://www.mckinsey.com/insights/consumer_and_retail/how_retailers_can_keep_up_with_consumers.

Malouff, Dan. "Walmart's 6 DC Stores: Some Will Be Urban, Some Won't." *Greater Washington* blog, April 26, 2012. http://greatergreaterwashington.org/post/14555/walmarts-6-dc-stores-some-will-be-urban-some-wont/.

Manners-Bell, John, and Ken Lyon. "The Implications of 3D Printing for the Global Logistics Industry." *Supplychain247,* January 23, 2014. http://www.supplychain247.com/article/the_implications_of_3d_printing_for_the_global_logistics_industry.

Marle, Gavin Van. "A New Era for Supply Chains As Faster IT Systems Push Data into the Driving Seat." *Loadstar,* September 16, 2014. http://theloadstar.co.uk/intel-gartner-gt-nexus-future-supply-chains-procurement/.

Mattoo, Aaditya, Robert M. Stern, and Gianni Zanini, eds. *A Handbook of International Trade in Services.* Oxford: Oxford University Press, 2007.

Miller, Claire Cain, and Stephanie Clifford. "E-Commerce Companies Bypass the Middlemen." *New York Times,* March 31, 2013. http://www.nytimes.com/2013/04/01/business/e-commerce-companies-bypass-middlemen-to-build-premium-brand.html?pagewanted=all.

Morgan Stanley Research. "eCommerce Disruption: A Global Theme," January 6, 2013.

National Bureau of Economic Research (NBER). "U.S. Business Cycle Expansions and Contractions." http://www.nber.org/cycles.html (accessed November 17, 2014).

Pilat, Dirk. "Regulation and Performance in the Distribution Services Sector." Paris: Organization for Economic Co-operation and Development (OECD), 1997. http://www.oecd.org/eco/reform/1864037.pdf.

Scheyder, Ernest. "Analysis: U.S. Ports' Drive to Control Costs Leads to Labor Strife." Reuters, January 17, 2013. http://www.reuters.com/article/2013/01/17/us-usa-ports-labor-idUSBRE90G06W20130117.

SelectUSA. "The Logistics and Transportation Industry in the United States." n.d. http://selectusa.commerce.gov/industry-snapshots/logistics-and-transportation-industry-united-states (accessed November 18, 2014).

Stynes, Tess. "Union Pacific Profit Rises 19% on Freight Traffic Growth." *Wall Street Journal,* October 23, 2014. http://www.wsj.com/articles/union-pacific-profit-rises-19-on-freight-traffic-growth-1414067300.

U.S. Department of Commerce (USDOC). Bureau of Economic Analysis (BEA). *Guide to Industry Classifications for International Surveys, 2007,* December 2007. http://www.bea.gov/surveys/iftcmat.htm.

———. "Real Value Added by Industry." Interactive tables: Gross Domestic Product by Industry Accounts, November 13, 2014. http://www.bea.gov/iTable/iTable.cfm?ReqID=51&step=1#reqid=51&step=2&isuri=1 (accessed November 17, 2014).

———. *Survey of Current Business 90,* no. 10 (October 2010).

———. *Survey of Current Business 94,* no. 10 (October 2014).

———. Table 6.3D: "Wage and Salary Accruals per Full Time Equivalent Employee by Industry." Interactive tables: National and Product Accounts, August 5, 2014. http://www.bea.gov/iTable/iTable.cfm?ReqID=9&step=1#reqid=9&step=3&isuri=1&904=2008&903=197&906=q&905=2013&910=x&911=0 (accessed November 17, 2014).

———. Table 6.5D, "Full-Time Equivalent Employees by Industry." Interactive tables: Gross Domestic Product by Industry Accounts, August 5, 2014. http://www.bea.gov/iTable/iTable.cfm?ReqID=9&step=1#reqid=9&step=3&isuri=1&904=2008&903=197&906=q&905=2013&910=x&911=0 (accessed November 17, 2014).

———. Table 6.6D, "Wages and Salaries per Full-Time Equivalent Employees by Industry." Interactive tables: Gross Domestic Product by Industry Accounts, August 5, 2014. http://www.bea.gov/iTable/iTable.cfm?ReqID=9&step=1#reqid=9&step=3&isuri=1&904=2008&903=201&906=q&905=2013&910=x&911=0 (accessed November 17, 2014).

U.S. International Trade Commission (USITC). *Digital Trade in the U.S. and Global Economies, Part 1*. USITC Publication 4415. Washington, DC: USITC, July 2013. http://www.usitc.gov/publications/332/pub4415.pdf.

World Trade Organization (WTO). "Distribution Services: Background Note by the Secretariat." S/C/W/326, October 29, 2010. https://docs.wto.org/dol2fe/Pages/FE_Search/DDFDocuments/76656/Q/S/C/W326.pdf.

———. "Sector By Sector: Distribution Services," n.d. http://www.wto.org/english/tratop_e/serv_e/distribution_e/distribution_e.htm (accessed October 7, 2014).

Chapter 3
Logistics Services

Summary

Logistics services are a vital tool of the modern supply chain, facilitating the transport and distribution of goods from producers to consumers. In 2013, the demand for logistics services was highest in markets where trade volume was most concentrated—namely, in economies with both a large consumer market and a substantial role in global supply chains. However, burdensome customs and border procedures and poor infrastructure development in some countries create high logistics costs, making it harder for logistics firms to operate efficiently.

Changes in market forces, such as consumption patterns, production costs, and new technologies, are compressing global supply chains into regional networks. E-commerce is the driving demand factor for logistics services: as consumers increasingly buy products online, the need for additional storage facilities and express delivery carriers is growing. At the same time, global value chains are beginning to contract, as manufacturers relocate their production and assembly sites away from traditional hubs and establish supply networks closer to major markets to reduce transportation costs and protect against supply disruptions. Additionally, new technologies, such as 3-D printing, enable manufacturers to make products at a local facility without having to coordinate the transportation of multiple parts to a central assembly site. In response to these trends, logistics providers are focusing more on coordinating complete supply chains on a regional scale, and on efficiently managing inventory levels between distribution centers and retailers.

In 2013, total U.S. cross-border exports and imports in logistics services reached $42.1 billion, a 4.7 percent increase over the year before. Major U.S. trade partners in the industry continued to be China, Germany, Japan, the United Kingdom and France. Sales by foreign affiliates of U.S. logistics firms abroad grew faster than logistics services exports during 2008–12. During this period, affiliate sales grew by nearly 21 percent, compared to growth of less than 1 percent for U.S. cross-border exports of logistics services. The strong affiliate growth suggests that U.S. logistics firms were increasing their commercial presence in foreign markets where demand is high.

Introduction

Logistics services include a broad set of activities that manage the end-to-end transport of raw, intermediate, and final goods between suppliers, producers, and consumers.[73] These services include freight forwarding; multimodal transport (i.e., transport using multiple means, such as air, ship, truck, or rail); warehousing and storage; tracking and tracing; and customs brokerage. The logistics industry has expanded to provide value-added services as well, such as order fulfillment, product repair, supply chain management,[74] and, more recently, inventory management and returns processing.[75] Today, logistics services may be supplied by second-, third-, fourth-, or even fifth-party logistics (2PL, 3PL, 4PL, and 5PL) companies.[76] As these services become more integrated, logistics providers now focus not only on operating a fleet of vehicles for transport and delivery services, but also on providing supply-management services and business-related information technology (IT) consulting services.[77]

Third-party logistics (3PL) firms, which are the focus of this chapter, may offer some or all of the services listed above to meet consumer demand for more information-intensive services. However, the two key components of global 3PL services are international transportation management, such as freight forwarding and non-vessel-operating common carrier services,[78] and warehousing and distribution services.[79] 3PL firms often divide their business into separate operating units that include air freight, sea freight, road and rail transport, and contract logistics services.[80] Markets for 3PL services are growing with the continuing global economic

---

[73] USITC, *Logistics Services: An Overview*, May 2005, 2-1.

[74] Supply chain management refers to the design and management of transportation and distribution networks, and may include software implementation and inventory management.

[75] Millar, "Reverse Logistics," July 30, 2014; DHL, *Annual Report 2013*, 2014, 25.

[76] CCB International Securities Ltd., "China Logistics," August 4, 2014, 14. A second-party logistics provider specializes in transportation services for the supply chain and generally operates an asset-based courier business, which means it owns or leases its own trucks, ships, or planes. Third-party providers offer transportation services as well, but their services also include warehousing, customs brokerage, and supply chain management. A fourth-party logistics provider, or lead logistics provider, manages the activities of all contracted second- and third-party providers that a company may employ using a single, integrated system. Finally, fifth-party logistics providers plan and execute complete supply chain strategies on behalf of their customers, offering system-based consulting services. Van Leeuwen, "1PL to 5PL: The Differences," June 17, 2014.

[77] DHL, "Definition of Contract Logistics," n.d. (accessed November 25, 2014).

[78] A non-vessel-operating common carrier buys cargo space at wholesale rates from shipping lines and resells the space at retail prices to shippers.

[79] Armstrong & Associates, "Global and Regional Infrastructure," January 2014, 14.

[80] While defined differently across firms and organizations, contract logistics generally refers to the value-added supply chain services that are distinct from transportation or freight-forwarding services and are more tailored to the needs of a logistics customer. These services are often industry-specific, such as special product packaging or repair and return services, and provided for a predetermined period of time.

recovery.[81] According to a 2013 Gartner report,[82] about 87 percent of companies contract a part of their supply chain services to 3PL providers, and 65 percent are increasing their usage of 3PL services.[83] Even multinational conglomerates that handle the majority of their supply chain services in-house, such as Walmart and Toyota, may outsource a part of their logistics needs to a 3PL firm if they can save on costs as a result.

Market Conditions in Global Third-Party Logistics (3PL) Services

The flow of merchandise trade strongly influences the flow of global freight traffic and logistics services. To illustrate, in 2013, global merchandise trade grew by only 2.2 percent, and 3PL revenues similarly increased by a modest 2.7 percent to $703.8 billion (table 3.1).[84] By contrast, from 2008 to 2012, 3PL revenues grew at robust rates in regions such as Asia and Latin America. During this period, total merchandise trade grew 13.0 percent in Asia, and 3PL revenues rose 19.8 percent; in Latin America, merchandise trade jumped 13.4 percent and 3PL revenues also grew substantially at 28.5 percent.[85]

Table 3.1: Third-party logistics (3PL) revenues, by country

Country	2013 revenue (billions $)	Global share (%)	Growth rate 2012–2013
United States	146.4	20.8	3.2
China	127.4	18.1	7.6
Japan	54.3	7.7	2.1
Germany	31.7	4.5	0.6
France	26.0	3.7	0.0
Brazil	25.6	3.6	2.4
United Kingdom	22.8	3.2	1.3
Italy	20.4	2.9	-1.9
India	17.4	2.5	4.8
Australia	16.9	2.4	2.4
Canada	16.9	2.4	1.8
World total	703.8		

Source: Armstrong & Associates, Inc. (accessed October 2, 2014).

---

[81] Capgemini and Langley, *2014 Third-Party Logistics Study,* 2014, 10.

[82] Gartner, Inc., is an IT research and advisory company that produces for-fee industry reports, such as the annual *Magic Quadrant for Global Third-Party Logistics Providers,* May 12, 2014.

[83] WTO, *World Trade Report 2014,* 18; Marle, "Major Shippers Moving Towards 3PLs," September 15, 2014.

[84] Estimates are based on data purchased from Armstrong & Associates.

[85] Logistics estimates are based on data purchased from Armstrong & Associates and data from WTO, Time Series on International Trade, n.d. (accessed December 11, 2014).

There was little change between 2012 and 2013 in the composition of the top 10 providers of logistics services. The United States, China, and Japan remained the largest suppliers of 3PL services, accounting for nearly 47 percent of revenue in the global 3PL market. Most of the top 10 3PL countries recorded small 3PL revenue increases from 2012 to 2013,[86] although China substantially outpaced other countries with 7.6 percent growth in 3PL revenues in 2013, reflecting an increase in merchandise trade of 7.5 percent during that year. Australia broke into the top 10 in 2013, sharing the 10th spot with Canada. These countries accounted for 2.4 percent each of global 3PL revenues in 2013.

3PL service providers are also active in developing economies. Together, Brazil, China, and India accounted for about $170.4 billion up 6.5 percent from 2012, or 24.2 percent of global 3PL revenue in 2013. In 2013, India overtook Canada to become the ninth-largest provider in third-party logistics services, with $17.4 billion in revenue. Other developing countries such as Bangladesh, Cambodia, Laos, Burma, and Vietnam are also establishing their presence in global supply networks, particularly as suppliers of low-cost manufacturing.[87] For example, Vietnam is one of the fastest-growing air cargo markets globally, in large part due to the presence of large-scale manufacturers like Samsung, LG Electronics, and Apple. Such manufacturers often rely on air freight to quickly transport high-value intermediate goods, including computer parts.[88]

Overall, 3PL firms primarily serve the high-tech, automotive, and retail industries. In 2013, these three industries represented the largest revenue sources for 3PL firms, accounting for about 61 percent of total global Fortune 500 spending on 3PL usage.[89] However, logistics services for healthcare and pharmaceutical products have also seen sustained demand, recording 9.1 percent annual growth between 2008 and 2012.[90] For example, Germany-based Kuehne + Nagel, a leading global logistics firm, reported above-average growth in its pharmaceutical and healthcare business lines in 2013 with the launch of its KN PharmaChain, an air cargo service that provides temperature-controlled delivery using remote-sensor technology.[91]

---

[86] The exception was Italy, the seventh-largest 3PL provider in 2013, which posted $20.4 billion in revenue, down 1.9 percent from the previous year.

[87] Lennane, "IAG Cargo Says 'Structural Change,'" September 25, 2014.

[88] Boudreau, "Jets Depart Saigon Belly Full," November 12, 2014.

[89] Estimates are based on data purchased from Armstrong & Associates, "Trends in 3PL/Customer Relationships 2013," July 2013.

[90] Estimates are based on data purchased from Armstrong & Associates (accessed November 12, 2014).

[91] Kuehne + Nagel, *2013 Annual Report,* 2014, 26–27. Remote-sensor technology, such as radar or satellite imaging, is a method of getting information about the properties of a specified object from a distance, without coming into contact with it. In this case, remote sensors obtain and relay information on the temperature of pharmaceutical goods during transport. Hoang and Caudill, "Remote Sensing," n.d. (accessed December 15, 2014).

3PL Logistics Costs are High in Developing Economies despite Promising Revenue Growth

The amount that a country spends on logistics services as a percentage of its GDP—its "logistics expenditure ratio"—is another way to measure performance in 3PL markets.[92] A high ratio may signal inefficiencies in a country's logistics market as a result of inadequate transportation infrastructure or a poor customs environment.[93] In 2013, under this measurement, the Netherlands was the most efficient market in the global 3PL industry, with a logistics expenditure ratio of 8.3. The United States, Japan, Hong Kong, and Singapore followed closely, each with a ratio of 8.5. According to this metric, the most inefficient logistics markets in 2013 were all emerging economies; China, India, and Brazil each recorded logistics expenditure ratios of over 10 percent of their GDP.[94] Logistics costs in the Asia-Pacific region, including China, the region's largest 3PL market, are sufficiently high to dampen the competitiveness of Asia's logistics providers (figure 3.1). Despite recent consolidation efforts in the industry, the Chinese logistics market remains deeply fragmented, leading to inefficiency and low profitability.[95] For example, strong competition between state and private express carriers in the local delivery market is reducing marginal revenue per package, and the predominance of small firms with limited infrastructure networks add to high operating costs.[96] Likewise, ongoing challenges in Brazil, such as poor transportation networks and burdensome customs procedures, have created high logistics costs relative to nearby markets. As a result, some automobile manufacturers, such as Audi and Mercedes, have chosen to invest in new production facilities in Mexico, for example, because its logistics costs and processes are currently more competitive than in Brazil.[97]

---

[92] The logistics expenditure ratio is a useful but imperfect measure of a country's logistics efficiency. For further discussion, see Shepherd, "Logistics Costs and Competitiveness," 2011, 5–7.

[93] Armstrong & Associates, *Global and Regional Infrastructure,* January 2014, 4.

[94] Estimates are based on data purchased from Armstrong & Associates (accessed October 2, 2014).

[95] CCB International Securities Ltd., "China Logistics," August 4, 2014, 2.

[96] Millar, "China Logistics Stretched by Exponential Growth," October 6, 2014; Fung Business Intelligence Centre, "Logistics Industry in China," August 2013, 21.

[97] Ludwig, "South America Summit," November 5, 2014; PricewaterhouseCoopers, *Transportation and Logistics 2030,* 2010, 32.

Figure 3.1: The Asia-Pacific region (including China) recorded the highest global logistics costs in 2013

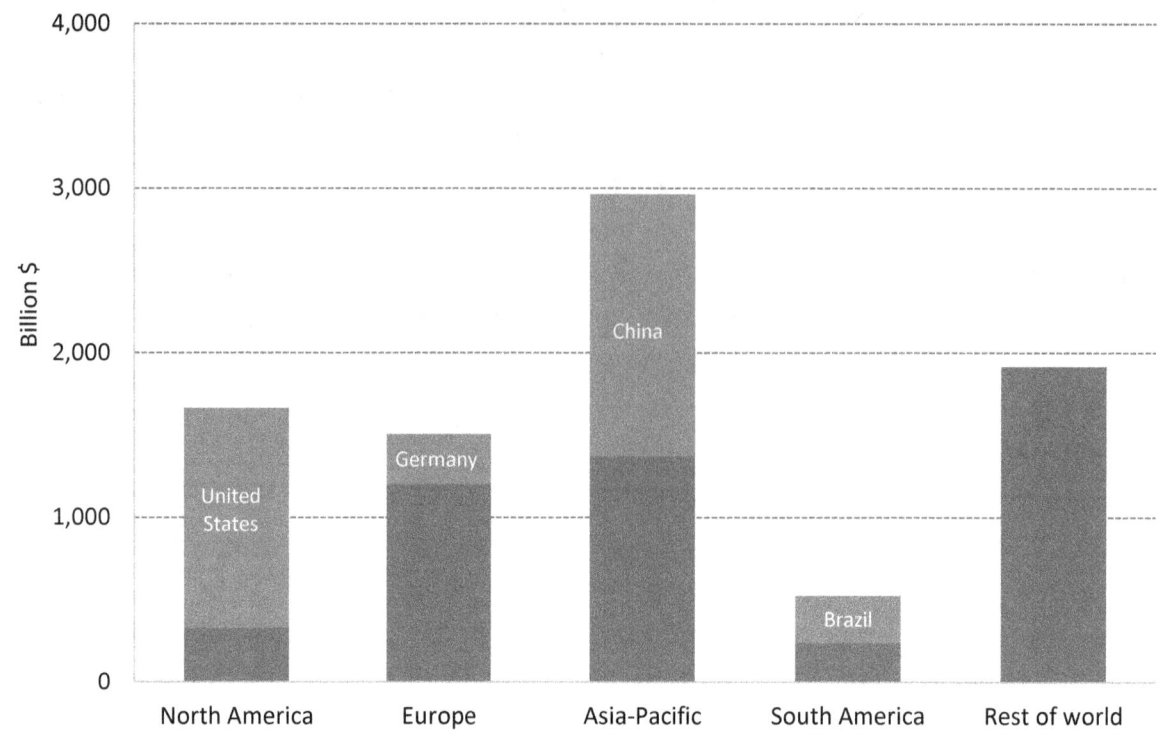

Source: Armstrong & Associates (accessed October 2, 2014). (See appendix table B.7).

Revenues of Leading 3PL Providers Fell in 2013, Although Some Segments Remained Profitable

In 2013, weak global economic activity and slow growth in international trade continued to depress 3PL revenues for the industry's leading firms. The total revenue of the top 10 global firms has been stagnant or declining since 2008, even though the global logistics market as a whole reported annual growth of 8.1 percent between 2008 and 2012.[98] These top 10 firms represented about 20 percent of global market revenues in 2013, down from a share of close to 30 percent in 2008 (table 3.2).[99] According to annual reports, some firms' revenue fell short of expectations in 2013 due to a decline in freight volumes, decreasing logistics demand in certain regions, or negative currency effects.[100]

---

[98] Estimates are based on data purchased from Armstrong & Associates (accessed September 15, 2014).

[99] The top 10 firms in 2013 are not the same as the top 10 firms in 2008. Estimates are based on data purchased from Armstrong & Associates (accessed September 15, 2014).

[100] DHL, *Annual Report 2013,* 2014, 49; Kuehne + Nagel, *2013 Annual Report,* 2014, 15; DB Schenker Logistics, *Annual Report,* 2013, 166.

Table 3.2: Top 10 global third-party logistics (3PLs), by revenue

Company	2013 Revenue (millions $)	Headquarters	Global market share (%)	Primary industry
DHL Supply Chain & Global Forwarding	31,432	Germany	4.5	Retail, consumer, IT, health
Kuehne + Nagel	22,587	Switzerland	3.2	Automotive, healthcare, IT, retail
DB Schenker Logistics	19,732	Germany	2.8	Automotive, electronics, consumer, healthcare
Nippon Express	17,317	Japan	2.5	Automotive, healthcare, computers and electronics
C.H. Robinson Worldwide	12,752	United States	1.8	Technology, food and beverage, retail, ag
CEVA Logistcs	8,517	Netherlands	1.2	Automotive, retail, industrial, technology
DSV	8,140	Denmark	1.2	Automotive, industrial, retail
Sinotrans	7,738	China	1.1	Automotive, IT, retail
Panalpina	7,293	Switzerland	1.0	Automotive, computers and electronics, consumer, apparel, healthcare
SDV (Bollore Group)	7,263	France	1.0	Automotive, IT, food and beverage
Total	142,771		20.3	
Grand total	703,800		100	

Source: Armstrong & Associates, Inc. (accessed September 15, 2014), JOC.com (accessed November 3, 2014), Foster and Armstrong, "Top 25 Third-Party Logistics Providers," (accessed November 3, 2014), and annual reports.

The top 10 global firms in 3PL services are broadly diversified and generally offer the complete spectrum of logistics services, including value-added services, such as supply chain consulting and order processing. While transportation management and freight-forwarding services are core activities for the majority of these firms, declining revenue in these service segments was partially offset by growth in other, non-core areas. For example, between 2012 and 2013, revenues in DHL's air and ocean freight businesses fell by about 10 percent and 5 percent, respectively. However, DHL's mail segment posted 3.4 percent revenue growth over the same period.[101] Similarly, freight-forwarding revenue for DB Schenker fell 8.0 percent in 2013, compared with a 5.2 percent increase in revenues for its contract logistics business.[102]

---

[101] DHL, *Annual Report 2013,* 2014, 62.
[102] Armstrong & Associates, "Trends in 3PL/Customer Relationships—2013," July 2013, 18.

Emerging Demand and Supply Factors

Three key drivers in the 3PL services market are shifting the landscape of global supply chains and reshaping the function of transportation and storage service providers. The following discussion outlines the roles that e-commerce, near-shoring, and new technologies play in the demand and supply of global logistics services.

E-commerce Creates More Demand for 3PL Services

E-commerce has become the most important driver of growth in logistics services.[103] In fact, with customers like Amazon, Drugstore.com, and Google, Internet retailing services is one of the fastest-growing 3PL revenue subsegments.[104] Online shopping is changing the traditional supply chain,[105] and retailers are adjusting to the demand by shrinking their distribution networks and building more local hubs to improve express delivery capabilities, such as two-day shipping. As more consumers buy online, retailers increasingly use 3PL service providers to move their products. As a result, global supply networks are seeing shorter transport distances, increases in less-than-truckload deliveries,[106] higher volume for regional package carriers, and placement of warehouses and distribution centers closer to consumers.[107]

An important part of the e-commerce trend is the growing online presence of small and medium-sized enterprises (SMEs), which are expected to account for an increasing share of 3PL spending.[108] Many SMEs now maintain only an online retail site, often via leading e-commerce platforms such as Amazon, Alibaba, and eBay, and forego a traditional storefront to keep costs low and access a wider consumer base. According to a joint study conducted by DHL and the Economist Intelligence Unit, most SMEs expect to receive as much as half of their revenue from international sales, which will likely be met through online orders.[109] In addition, based on annual trends in 3PL customer relationships, smaller companies have shown the largest increases in 3PL usage since 2008, meaning that SMEs are continuing to outsource more logistics functions to 3PLs.[110] For example, the partnership between DHL and German-based

---

[103] DHL, *Annual Report 2013,* 2014, 25. E-commerce is also discussed later in chapter 5, "Retail Services."

[104] Armstrong & Associates, "Trends in 3PL/Customer Relationships—2013," July 2013, 10.

[105] PR Newswire, "Digital Logistics Market by System and by Service," September 15, 2014.

[106] "Less than truckload" refers to shipments that are smaller than a full truckload and are often consolidated with other shipments into one load for transport. DHL, *Annual Report 2013*, 2014, 218.

[107] Georgia Center for Innovation Logistics, *2013 Georgia Logistics Report: A Global Perspective,* 109; Supply Chain Matters, "Trends That Will Shape the Supply Chain," January 28, 2014.

[108] Armstrong & Associates, "Trends in 3PL/Customer Relationships—2013," July 2013, 6.

[109] Chaney, "Breaking Borders: From Canada to China," 2014.

[110] Armstrong & Associates, "Trends in 3PL/Customer Relationships—2013," July 2013, 5–6.

retailer Zalando has allowed the small online fashion store to focus its resources on expanding product lines and selling to customers outside of Germany, while DHL handles domestic and international deliveries, warehouse logistics, and other support services.[111]

Recent growth in e-commerce is especially evident in China, a country increasingly recognized as a growing consumer power.[112] Because tier-3 cities[113] or remote regions like western China have few brick-and-mortar retailers, consumers in these regions tend to shop online. Also driving e-commerce demand is China's growing middle class. Mid- to high-income consumers find that e-tailers[114] offer a larger variety of products to satisfy evolving tastes.[115] Given the industry's exponential growth, analysts expect the logistical requirements of e-commerce to push up the value of China's logistics industry and project this figure to reach $45.5 billion (RMB 280 billion)[116] by 2015, which would require an annual growth rate of almost 40 percent.[117] In fact, online sales in China have risen by an average of 31 percent over the last year (2013), driven principally by the purchase of automotive, food, and luxury items.[118] Moreover, the share of China's online sales volume as a percentage of the country's total retail sales volume grew from about 1 percent in 2008 to 8 percent in 2013.[119]

In China as elsewhere, expanding e-commerce requires building more fulfillment and distribution centers closer to customers. Consequently, land supply for storage and warehouses, a growing issue in the global logistics industry, has become a major concern in China's first-tier cities,[120] where both brick-and-mortar and e-commerce companies need more distribution space. Access to land in China is further complicated by district governments' preference for allocating space to manufacturing industries, which generate higher tax

---

[111] DHL, *Annual Report 2013,* 2014, 10–12.

[112] Deloitte, "Business Trends 2014: Navigating the Next Wave," 2014, 82; Millar, "China Logistics Stretched by Exponential Growth," October 6, 2014.

[113] "Tier-3" (or third-tier) is a term used to refer to cities in China, such as Hangzhou and Chongqing, with low economic and infrastructure development but with some cultural significance. By comparison, first-tier cities, like Beijing, Shanghai, and Guangzhou, tend to be the most developed and to also have important historical relevance. American Chamber of Commerce in Shanghai, "What Is Meant by First-Tier?" n.d. http://sme.amcham-shanghai.org/faq/what-meant-first-tier-second-tier-and-third-tier-cities (accessed December 1, 2014).

[114] E-tailing (or e-retailing) and e-tailer are industry terms that refer to online retailing and retailers (a growing phenomenon).

[115] Millar, "China Logistics Stretched by Exponential Growth," October 6, 2014.

[116] Based on the 2013 yuan/$ exchange rate of 6.15. Federal Reserve, "Foreign Exchange Rates—G.5A," January 2, 2014, http://www.federalreserve.gov/releases/G5a/current/default.htm.

[117] Millar, "China Logistics Stretched by Exponential Growth," October 6, 2014; CCB International Securities, "China Logistics," August 4, 2014, 3.

[118] Qazi, "China's New Open Door," October 2, 2014.

[119] CCB International Securities, "China Logistics," August 4, 2014, 11.

[120] CCB International Securities, "China Logistics," August 4, 2014, 16; Armstrong & Associates, "Trending Up: 3PL Market Predictions," July 2014, 4.

revenues.[121] Additionally, 3PL providers operating in the Chinese market need to significantly increase their fleet of delivery trucks and motorcycles to continue to meet the delivery demand created by e-commerce.[122]

Near-shoring and Digital Technologies have the Potential to Change the Types of Services 3PL Providers Supply

Near-shoring[123]—the recent phenomenon of firms relocating manufacturing facilities and services closer to consumer markets—is affecting the structure of modern supply chains, leading 3PL providers to adjust their service offerings in response. Manufacturers are near-shoring to protect their network from global supply disruptions and to reduce transport costs.[124] Proximity to major consumer markets also allows firms to monitor inventory levels and gives them more flexibility to respond to demand and supply changes.[125] Instead of supply chains linking production sites around the world, top firms are developing complete regional networks around high-growth markets, such as Asia. As a result, "optimized" supply chains that once focused on minimizing systemwide inventory costs are evolving into "adaptive" and "anticipatory" supply chains, more focused on managing risk, increasing flexibility, and better absorbing supply-side shocks, such as natural disasters.[126] Shorter distances between producer and consumer may also lessen demand for freight-forwarding services while requiring more value-added services in terms of inventory management, subassembly, and reverse logistics.[127]

---

[121] Knowler, "Land Access Remains Key Issue," November 21, 2014.

[122] Szakonyi, "Asia's Big Logistics Picture," October 27, 2014, 36–37.

[123] Increasing wage and other production costs in traditionally low-cost countries, such as China, have encouraged global manufacturing firms to move production closer to consumer markets. DHL Trend Research, "Logistics Trend Radar," 2014, 28.

[124] In a 2014 survey of U.S. manufacturers and distributors, Alixpartners, a global consulting group, found that 67 percent of respondents expected to move their products faster to markets as a result of near-shoring, and 59 percent expected to see lower freight costs. AlixPartners, "2014 Reshoring/Nearshoring Executive Survey and Outlook," May 2014.

[125] Deloitte, "Business Trends 2014: Navigating the Next Wave," 2014, 82; Georgia Center for Innovation Logistics, *2013 Georgia Logistics Report: A Global Perspective,* March 17, 2013, 6.

[126] Deloitte, "Business Trends 2014: Navigating the Next Wave," 2014, 78–80.

[127] Reverse logistics includes logistics services that are provided after a product is delivered to the consumer, primarily coordinating the return or repair of a product to the retailer or manufacturer. Cerasis, "What Is Reverse Logistics?" February 19, 2014.

At the same time, trends vary by industry: pharmaceuticals are actually sourcing from further away as "cold-chain" logistics services become more advanced.[128]

New technologies, such as delivery drones,[129] big data analytics, and 3-D printing, are also affecting the types of services that 3PL firms provide. Key to a number of new industry technologies, "big data analytics" are being used by many 3PL providers to improve operational efficiency and deliver innovative solutions to consumers (box 3.1). However, among these technologies, 3-D printing[130] is a trend that may have the strongest, most immediate impact on the logistics industry.[131] Shorter product cycles, particularly of high-tech and electronic goods, are likely to result from manufacturing multiple parts in a single central assembly site. This process will require less transportation during production and reduce the need for long-distance shipping.[132] In fact, near-shoring the production of more goods from developing markets back to North America and Europe would change the scale of 3PL services activities.[133] The use of compact but comprehensive 3-D manufacturing facilities will reduce freight shipping and warehousing requirements, forcing 3PL providers to evolve more of their services into vendor management, network design and development, and process engineering.[134] Adapting to these changes, some 3PL providers such as UPS are offering 3-D printing services themselves. Many of their customers are SMEs, such as entrepreneurs, engineers, and home inventors, for whom access to fast, accurate production of parts and prototypes is convenient and time-saving.[135]

---

[128] Transport Intelligence, "Stifel Logistics Confidence Index October 2014," October 16, 2014, 1; Lennane, "Air Freight Will Be Critical," December 16, 2014. A cold chain logistics network is a temperature-controlled transport system built to maintain optimum conditions for goods. 3PL providers are continuing to expand their activities and services in this field. For example, United Airlines Cargo offers TempControl services, using new battery-powered "e1" containers that they say customers prefer to dry ice. Roebuck, "United Boxing Clever," November 19, 2014.

[129] Increasingly popular in the courier express sector, delivery drones are driverless, aerial vehicles that are considered convenient for transporting packages to remote or congested areas. DHL Trend Research, "Logistics Trend Radar," 2014, 32.

[130] Manners-Bell and Lyon, "The Implications of 3D Printing for the Global Logistics Industry," August 2012, 1. 3-D printing, also known as "additive printing," is an automated method of producing prototypes that uses computer design to place layer on top of layer of materials, such as plastic, ceramic, or metal, until a finished good is produced. This kind of production may transform manufacturing by shifting it from hardware-based to software-dependent processes. See also Ford, "Additive Manufacturing Technology: Potential Implications for U.S. Manufacturing Competitiveness," September 2014.

[131] DHL Trend Research, "Logistics Trend Radar," 2014, 15.

[132] Cooke, "Three Trends to Watch in 2014," Quarter 4, 2013; Supply Chain Matters, "Trends That Will Shape the Supply Chain," January 28, 2014; Deloitte, "Business Trends 2014: Navigating the Next Wave," 2014, 82.

[133] DHL Trend Research, "Logistics Trend Radar," 2014, 4.

[134] Manners-Bell and Lyon, "The Implications of 3D Printing ," August 2012, 3–4.

[135] Supply Chain Matters, "The UPS Store Expands 3D Printing," October 1, 2014; Roebuck, "Onward and Upward for UPS in Europe," September 29, 2014.

Box 3.1: Major 3PL services providers are using big data analytics to bring innovative solutions to their customers

"Big data" refers to the large amounts of both quantitative and qualitative data that are now available to industry, often in real time, with the advent of advanced digital technologies.[a] For example, the 3PL logistics market uses big data to calculate estimated times of arrival (ETAs), product inventory levels, and capacity monitoring. Big data may also be used to design optimal transport routes, streamline inventory management, and ultimately reduce operating costs,[b] potentially offering firms a substantial competitive advantage.[c]

The logistics industry is combining big data analytics with social media networks to serve customers better, setting up online platforms where real-time data such as package tracking and delivery status can be accessed and shared by multiple parties.[d] For example, a new crowdsourcing program, MyWays, is an online social media application offering DHL customers control over package delivery. Using this program, a DHL customer who is a MyWays member can offer to transport a package for another MyWays member on a route that the former normally takes.[e] Through the use of such applications, 3PL firms may be better able to meet delivery times convenient for their customers, while reducing their transport costs at the same time.

Big data analytics can also help companies to streamline inventory management. For example, L'Oreal deployed a new data-monitoring system, MyPos, to improve visibility of inventory levels on retailers' shelves so that in-demand products were more readily available to consumers and low-selling products were not reordered.[f] Omnichannel retailing is an emerging distribution approach among retailers that integrates their online and brick-and-mortar shops (channels) into a single system. Combining management of online and offline purchases makes inventory management more efficient and allows companies to respond quickly to changes in market demand, often lowering their costs.[g]

Finally, big data is helping 3PL firms to reduce costs through enhanced ETA capabilities. Up-to-the-minute arrival and departure times are available through modern GPS tracking technology. More accurate ETAs can help freight forwarders synchronize transshipment schedules and mitigate losses due to missed connections, in particular for time-sensitive perishable goods. Examples are automatic identification systems, primarily used by ships. Connected via a GPS device and a transmitter, a ship transmits its real-time GPS data to a receiving station, like a satellite, that delivers the information to an online platform, such as MarineTraffic.com. Vessel ETAs and route forecasts can be accessed by freight forwarders, logistics managers, and shippers.[h]

[a] For more information on big data analytics, please consult two previous USITC reports, Digital Trade in the U.S. and Global Economies, Part 1, July 2013, and Digital Trade in the U.S. and Global Economies, Part 2, September 2014.
[b] Supply Chain Matters, "Trends that Will Shape the Supply Chain," January 28, 2014.
[c] Marle, "A New Era for Supply Chains," September 16, 2014.
[d] Rusch, "Using Social Media in the Supply Chain," August 6, 2014. MyWays only offers package monitoring, while DHL delivers the actual products.
[e] Supply Chain Matters, "Trends that Will Shape the Supply Chain," January 28, 2014.
[f] Marle, "L'Oreal Completes Five-Year Supply Chain Transformation," September 10, 2014.
[g] DHL, Annual Report 2013, 2014.
[h] Stasinakis, "Logistics Providers Can See the Big Picture," August 20, 2014.

Trade Trends

Cross-border Trade

In 2013, U.S. cross-border exports of logistics services (box 3.2) totaled $23.9 billion and cross-border imports totaled $18.2 billion, creating a trade surplus of $5.7 billion (figure 3.2). The U.S. surplus in logistics services grew by about 28 percent from 2012 to 2013, albeit slower than the 40 percent rise recorded a year earlier. The United States registered a cross-border trade surplus in logistics services each year from 2009 through 2012.[136]

Box 3.2: An explanation of BEA data on cross-border trade and affiliate transactions in logistics services

Official data on cross-border trade in logistics services are unavailable. Data on trade in air freight transport services and airport services are therefore used as proxies, as they reflect a large portion of trade in logistics services. Cross-border trade in air freight transport and airport services is derived from merchandise trade, and thus frequently fluctuates with merchandise trade activity. To avoid any double-counting, maritime freight and port services have been excluded from this chapter's discussion of trade trends because they are discussed separately in chapter 4.

Cross-border trade in air freight transport services can be broken down into two components. The first—exports of air freight transport services—refers to the transport of U.S. merchandise on U.S. air carriers to foreign destinations or between foreign ports. The second—imports of air freight transport services—refers to the transport of goods to the United States by foreign air carriers.

Similarly, U.S. exports of airport services (which pertain to both freight and passenger services) reflect the value of goods (except fuel) and services procured by foreign carriers at U.S. airports, while imports of airport services reflect the value of goods and services procured by U.S. carriers at foreign airports.

Given the absence of official data on affiliate transactions in logistics services, BEA is unable to divide this information at the individual sector level. Therefore, data on transportation, including air, rail, and truck, as well as related support activities, such as warehousing, will serve as the best proxies. Thus, the BEA estimates include sales of all services by transportation and supporting affiliates, not just those pertaining directly to air transport and airport services.

---

[136] The analysis in this section is based on data found in USDOC, BEA, *Survey of Current Business*, October 2014, unless otherwise noted.

Figure 3.2: Logistics services: U.S. cross-border trade in logistics services resulted in a U.S. trade surplus each year during 2009–13

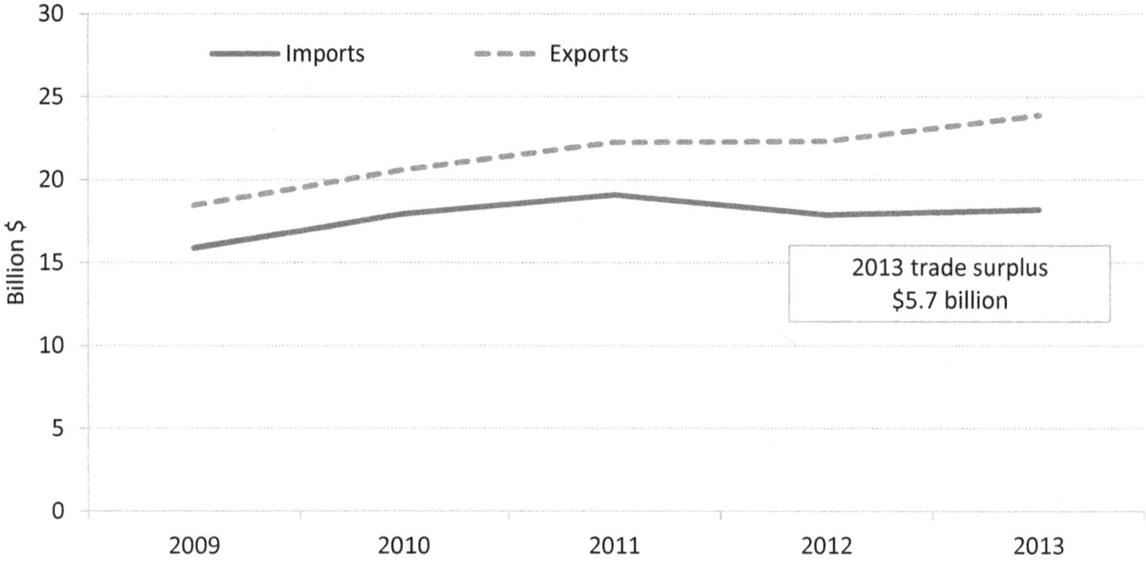

Source: USDOC, BEA, Survey of Current Business, October 2014, 1–2, table 1. (See appendix table B.8).

A slowdown in global economic activity following the financial crisis tempered growth in U.S. exports of logistics services beginning in 2009. As a result, U.S. exports in logistics services grew at an annual rate of only 0.5 percent during 2008–12, but increased by 7 percent in 2013.[137] The 2013 increase is primarily due to growth in U.S. exports of airport services, which outpaced growth in U.S. exports of air freight transport services that year by 10 percent. Air freight transport services accounted for approximately 60 percent of U.S. exports in logistics services in 2013, but grew by only 3.2 percent during this period, compared to 0.7 percent during 2008–12.[138] The relatively modest increase in U.S. exports of air freight transport services in the last few years likely reflects a shift towards less expensive modes of freight transportation, particularly ocean freight.[139]

In 2013, the United Kingdom was the largest single U.S. export market for logistics services, accounting for 17 percent of U.S. exports in the sector (figure 3.3).[140] Other major markets for U.S. logistics services in 2013 were Germany (7 percent), Japan (6 percent), China (5 percent),

---

[137] USDOC, BEA, *Survey of Current Business*, October 2014, 1–2, table 1.
[138] Ibid.
[139] Kirkeby, "Industry Surveys: Transportation: Commercial," February 2014, 3; Lennane, "We Must Cut 48 Hours Off Transit Times," October 8, 2014.
[140] USDOC, BEA, *Survey of Current Business*, October 2014, 6, table 3.2.

and Brazil (4 percent) (figure 3.4). In 2013, U.S. exports of logistics services to China and Japan were robust, which is likely due to continued growing demand for goods in these markets.[141]

Figure 3.3: Logistics services: In 2013, the United States posted its largest trade surplus in logistics services with the United Kingdom

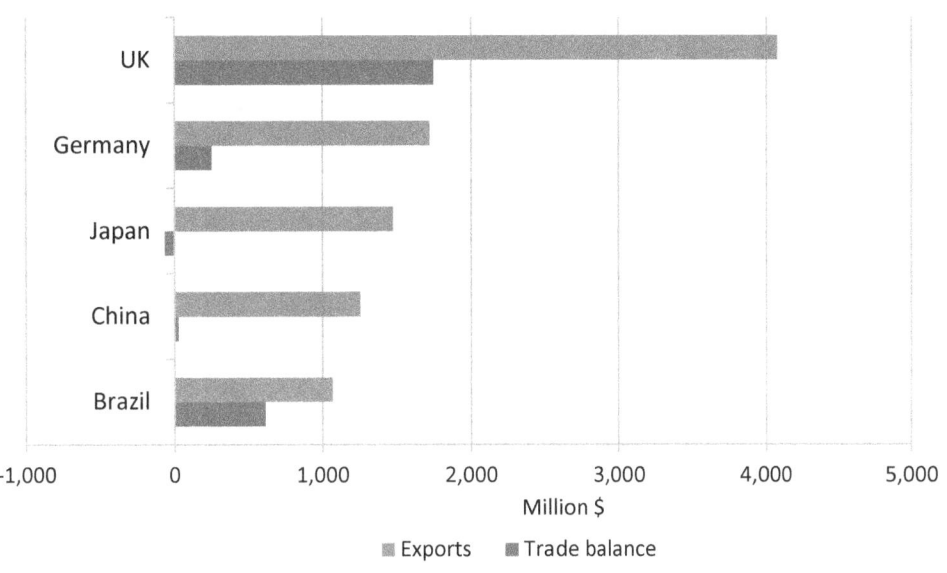

Source: USDOC, BEA, Survey of Current Business, October 2014, 6, table 3.2. (See appendix table B.9).

---

[141] In 2013, the United States had a small trade deficit in logistics services of $65 million with Japan. By contrast, during the same year, the United States had a trade surplus with China of $28 million (figure 3.3).

Figure 3.4: Logistics services: The United Kingdom was the leading market for U.S. cross-border exports and imports of logistics services in 2013

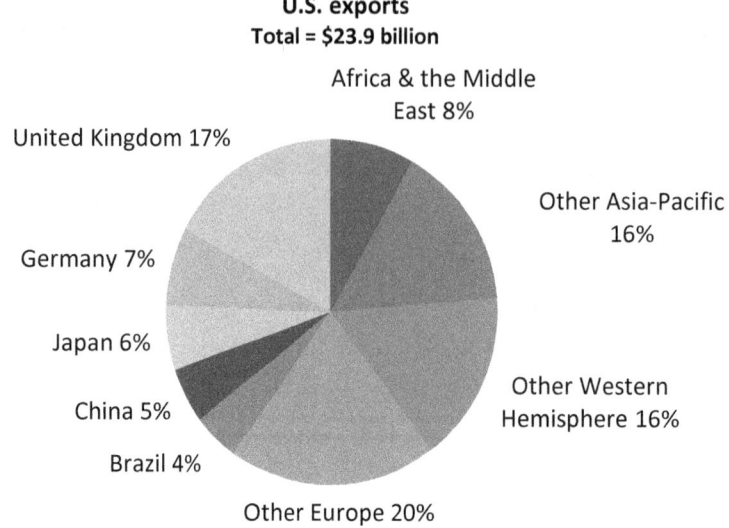

U.S. exports
Total = $23.9 billion

Africa & the Middle East 8%

United Kingdom 17%

Other Asia-Pacific 16%

Germany 7%

Japan 6%

China 5%

Other Western Hemisphere 16%

Brazil 4%

Other Europe 20%

U.S. imports
Total = $18.2 billion

Africa & the Middle East 6%

United Kingdom 13%

Other Europe 16%

Japan 8%

Germany 8%

Other Asia-Pacific 17%

China 7%

France 6%

Other Western Hemisphere 18%

Source: USDOC, BEA, *Survey of Current Business,* October 2014, 6, table 3.2. (See appendix table B.10).
Note: Figures may not total to 100 percent due to rounding.

U.S. imports of logistics services increased by 1.7 percent in 2013, compared to an annual decrease of 0.4 percent during 2008–12. In 2013, U.S. imports of airport services comprised more than 65 percent of total U.S. imports of logistics services. By country, the United Kingdom was the largest supplier of logistics services to the U.S. market, accounting for 13 percent of total U.S. cross-border imports of logistics services, followed by Japan and Germany (8 percent each), China (7 percent), and France (6 percent).[142] Overall, the Asia-Pacific region represents 32 percent of total U.S. imports of logistics services, less than the 43 percent share registered in Europe.

Affiliate Transactions

Based on available data, sales by U.S.-owned foreign affiliates (U.S. companies located abroad) exceeded sales by foreign-owned U.S. affiliates (foreign companies located in the United States) each year during 2009–12 (figure 3.5). Sales by U.S.-owned foreign affiliates peaked in 2011 at $20.1 billion, and grew at an average annual rate of nearly 21 percent between 2008 and 2012.[143] Although U.S. cross-border exports of logistics services have consistently surpassed sales by U.S.-owned foreign affiliates over this period, sales by U.S.-owned foreign affiliates have grown faster. This may suggest that U.S. logistics firms are responding to a growing demand for value-added services that are more efficiently provided through a commercial presence located at the source of the demand. For example, U.S. firm UPS currently operates two logistics hubs in China and plans to expand the scale of its services in-country to accommodate China's growing high-tech manufacturers. Such services may include transportation management and network coordination.[144]

---

[142] USDOC, BEA, *Survey of Current Business*, October 2014, 1–6, tables 1 and 3.2.

[143] USDOC, BEA, International Data, Interactive tables: "Table 3.1: Services Supplied to Foreign Persons by U.S. MNEs through Their MOFAs, by Industry of Affiliate and by Country of Affiliate," and "Table 4.1: Services Supplied to U.S. Persons by Foreign MNEs through Their MOUSA, by Industry of Affiliate and by Country of UBO," October 24, 2014.

[144] *China Daily,* "UPS Gears Up for Expanded Regional Traffic," November 13, 2014.

Figure 3.5: Logistics services: Services supplied by affiliates of U.S.-owned logistics services firms abroad exceeded services supplied by foreign-owned affiliates in the United States in 2012

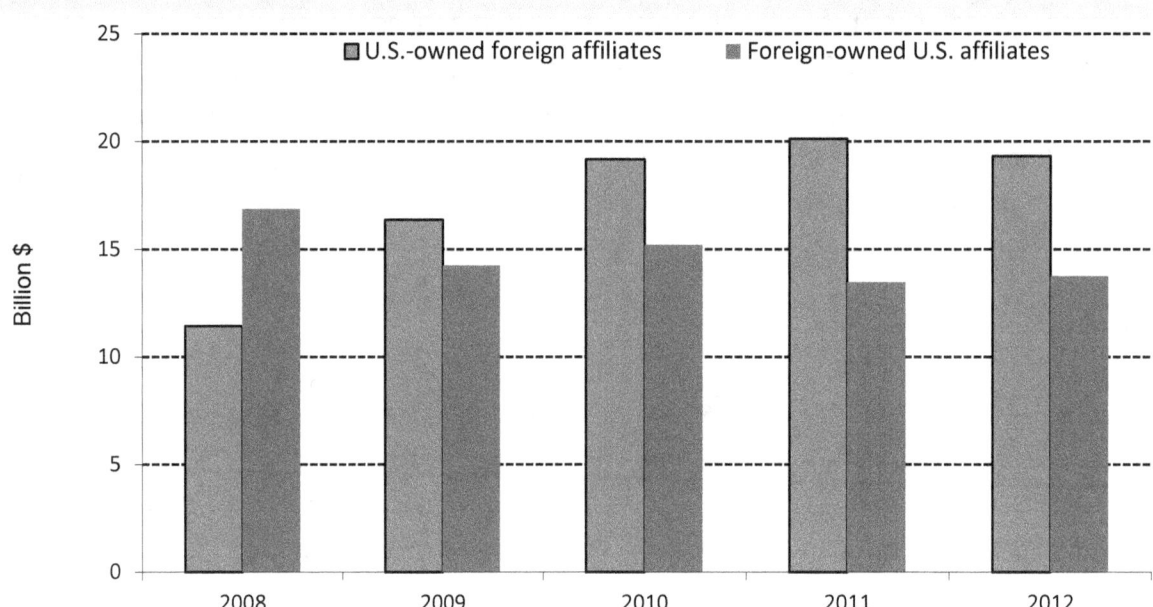

Source: USDOC, BEA, International Data, interactive tables: "Table 3.1: Services Supplied to Foreign Persons by U.S. MNEs through Their MOFAs, by Industry of Affiliate and by Country of Affiliate," and "Table 4.1: Services Supplied to U.S. Persons by Foreign MNEs through Their MOUSA, by Industry of Affiliate and by Country of UBO," October 24, 2014. (See appendix table B.11).

Note: Includes air transportation, rail transportation, truck transportation, and support activities for transportation. Totals for foreign-owned U.S. affiliates are underreported due to suppression of data to protect confidentiality.

Outlook

Continued growth in global merchandise trade in response to improving economic conditions will likely have a strong impact on the logistics industry.[145] In addition, the increasing concentration of supply chains within regional markets will affect the operations of 3PL providers. More concentrated supply chains will shorten transport distances between producers and consumers, and may allow more competition among different types of transportation services firms. For example, air transport services, which have typically been used for time-sensitive deliveries, may face more competition from other, less costly transport modes as manufacturers locate closer to export markets. Illustratively, in September 2013, the air freight industry reported a decrease in revenue ton-miles of 3.5 percent compared to the year before.[146] Given high freight rates, air cargo volumes are shifting to ocean shipping

---

[145] Yusof and Yap, "Global Industry Surveys: Airlines; Asia," January 2014, 2.

[146] A revenue ton-mile is the revenue that one ton of freight generates for each mile that it is transported. Revenue ton-miles are frequently used as a profitability indicator in the freight transport industry.

companies as a result of lower prices and improvements in ocean shippers' time-definite delivery services.[147]

China will likely continue to be an important growth market for logistics firms. China is currently the second-largest global logistics market and has shown robust growth since 2008; it is projected to surpass the United States as the world's largest 3PL market by 2016.[148] At the same time, China's domestic providers remain deeply fragmented, with the top 20 domestic 3PL firms in China accounting for only 7 percent of the Chinese logistics market.[149] As a result, the opportunity for U.S. and other leading 3PL firms to gain market share in China remains high.

---

[147] Kirkeby, "Industry Surveys: Transportation; Commercial," February 2014, 8.
[148] Millar, "China Logistics Sector Developments," September 1, 2014.
[149] Ibid.

Bibliography

AlixPartners. "2014 Reshoring/Nearshoring Executive Survey and Outlook," May 2014. http://www.alixpartners.com/en/Publications/AllArticles/tabid/635/articleType/Article View/articleId/1151/2014-ReshoringNearshoring-Executive-Survey-and-Outlook.aspx#sthash.XUnn1EXF.dpbs.

Armstrong & Associates. *Global and Regional Infrastructure, Logistics Costs, and Third-Party Logistics Market Trends and Analysis,* January 2014. http://www.3plogistics.com/Global_3PL_Market_Analysis_EIS-2014.pdf.

———. "Trending Up: 3PL Market Predictions for 2014 and 2013 Results," July 2014.

———. "Trends in 3PL/Customer Relationships—2013," July 2013.

———. Global 3PL Market Size Estimates. http://www.3plogistics.com/3PLmarketGlobal.htm (accessed various dates).

Boudreau, John. "Jets Depart Saigon Belly Full As Samsung Spurs Cargo Boom." Bloomberg, November 26, 2014. http://www.bloomberg.com/news/2014-11-10/jets-depart-saigon-belly-full-as-samsung-spurs-cargo-boom.html.

Capgemini and John Langley Jr. *2014 Third-Party Logistics Study: The State of Logistics Outsourcing,* 2014, 10. http://www.capgemini.com/resource-file-access/resource/pdf/3pl_study_report_web_version.pdf.

CCB International Securities Ltd. "China Logistics," August 4, 2014. http://www.kerrylogistics.com/sch/INVESTOR/analyst/images/20140804-CCBI-KerryLogistics-Initation.pdf.

Cerasis. "What Is Reverse Logistics and How Is It Different than Traditional Logistics?" February 19, 2014. http://cerasis.com/2014/02/19/what-is-reverse-logistics/.

Chaney, Joseph. "Breaking Borders: From Canada to China, Barriers Overshadow Growth for Expanding SMEs." Economist Intelligence Unit, 2014. http://www.economistinsights.com/sites/default/files/DHL%20-%20SME%20International%20trade%20-%20published.pdf.

Cooke, James A. "Three Trends to Watch in 2014." *Supply Chain Quarterly,* Quarter 4, 2013. http://www.supplychainquarterly.com/columns/20131215-three-trends-to-watch-in-2014/.

DB Schenker Logistics. *Deutsche Bahn 2013 Annual Report*, March 27, 2014. http://www1.deutschebahn.com/file/6806228/data/2013_dbgroup.pdf.

Deloitte. "Business Trends 2014: Navigating the Next Wave of Globalization." Deloitte University Press, 2014. http://d2mtr37y39tpbu.cloudfront.net/wp-content/uploads/2014/03/Business-Trends2014.pdf.

DHL Trend Research. "Logistics Trend Radar," 2014. http://www.dhl.com/en/about_us/logistics_insights/dhl_trend_research/trendradar.html.

———. Annual Report 2013, 2014. http://www.dpdhl.com/en/investors/financial_reports/annual_reports.html.

———. "Definition of Contract Logistics," n.d. http://www.dhldiscoverlogistics.com/cms/en/course/services/contract/contract_definition.jsp (accessed November 25, 2014).

Ford, Sharon. "Additive Manufacturing Technology: Potential Implications for U.S. Manufacturing Competitiveness," Journal of International Commerce and Economics, September 2014. http://www.usitc.gov/journals/Vol_VI_Article4_Additive_Manufacturing_Technology.pdf.

Foster, Thomas A., and Richard Armstrong. "Top 25 Third-Party Logistics Providers Extend Their Global Reach." SupplyChainBrain, n.d. http://www.supplychainbrain.com/content/sponsored-channels/kenco-logistic-services-third-party-logistics/single-article-page/article/top-25-third-party-logistics-providers-extend-their-global-reach/ (accessed November 3, 2014).

Fung Business Intelligence Centre. "Logistics Industry in China," August 2013. http://www.funggroup.com/eng/knowledge/research/china_dis_issue113.pdf.

Georgia Center for Innovation Logistics. 2013 Georgia Logistics Report: A Global Perspective. March 17, 2013. http://logistics.georgiainnovation.org/logistics-resources/annual-report.aspx.

Hoang, Bichlien, and Ashley Caudill. "Remote Sensing." IEEE Emerging Technology, n.d. (accessed December 15, 2014).

Kirkeby, Kevin. "Industry Surveys: Transportation; Commercial." Standard & Poor Capital IQ, February 2014.

Knowler, Greg. "Land Access Remains Key Issue for China Logistics Developers." Journal of Commerce, November 21, 2014. http://www.joc.com/international-logistics/land-access-remains-key-issue-china-logistics-developers_20141121.html.

Kuehne + Nagel. *2013 Annual Report,* 2014. http://www.kn-portal.com/fileadmin/user_upload/documents/about_us/Investor_Relations/documents/2013/annual_report/en/2013/index.html.

Lennane, Alex. "Air Freight Will Be Critical to New Trends in Pharmaceutical Supply Chains." *Loadstar,* December 16, 2014. http://theloadstar.co.uk/pharma-conference/.

———. "IAG Cargo Says 'Structural Change' Will Boost Shared Freighter Model." *Loadstar,* September 25, 2014. http://theloadstar.co.uk/air-freight-iag-atlas/.

———. "We Must Cut 48 Hours off Transit Times, or Air Cargo Cannot Survive." *Loadstar,* October 8, 2014. http://theloadstar.co.uk/aircargoforumday2/.

Ludwig, Christopher. "South America Summit: High Logistics Costs Put Brazil behind Mexico." *AutomotiveLogisticsMagazine.com,* November 5, 2014. http://www.automotivelogisticsmagazine.com/news/south-america-summit-high-logistics-costs-put-brazil-behind-mexico.

Manners-Bell, John, and Ken Lyon. "The Implications of 3D Printing for the Global Logistics Industry." Transport Intelligence, August 2012. http://www.transportintelligence.com/articles-papers/the-implications-of-3d-printing-for-the-global-logistics-industry/76.

Marle, Gavin Van. "A New Era for Supply Chains As Faster IT Systems Push Data into the Driving Seat." *Loadstar,* September 16, 2014. http://theloadstar.co.uk/intel-gartner-gt-nexus-future-supply-chains-procurement/.

———. "L'Oreal Completes Five-Year Supply Chain Transformation—'Because We're Worth It.'" *Loadstar,* September 10, 2014. http://theloadstar.co.uk/loreal-supply-chain-transformation/.

———. "Major Shippers Moving towards 3PLs As They Consolidate Their Logistics Providers." *Loadstar,* September 15, 2014. http://theloadstar.co.uk/gartner-third-party-logistics-provider-study/.

Millar, Mark. "China Logistics Sector Developments." Eyefortransport, September 1, 2014. http://www.eft.com/column/china-logistics-sector-developments.

———. "China Logistics Stretched by Exponential Growth in E-Commerce." Eyefortransport, October 6, 2014. http://www.eft.com/column/china-logistics-stretched-exponential-growth-e-commerce.

———. "Reverse Logistics—the Opportunities Outweigh the Challenges." Eyefortransport, July 30, 2014. http://www.eft.com/column/reverse-logistics-%E2%80%93-opportunities-outweigh-challenges.

Nippon Express. *Annual Report 2014*, August 2014.
http://nipponexpress.com/ir/library/annual/index.html.

PR Newswire. "Digital Logistics Market by System and by Service—Global Market Forecast and Analysis." News release, September 15, 2014. http://www.prnewswire.com/news-releases/digital-logistics-market-by-system-tracking--monitoring-information-integrated-edi-database-management-fleet-management-order-management-by-application-warehouse-transportation-labour-management--by-service---global-275161791.html.

PricewaterhouseCoopers. *Transportation & Logistics 2030.* Vol. 3, *Emerging Markets—New Hubs, New Spokes, New Industry Leaders?* 2010.
http://www.pwc.com/gx/en/transportationlogistics/tl2030/emerging-markets/new-hubs_new-spokes_new-industry-leaders.jhtml.

Qazi, Shehzad H. "China's New Open Door: The E-Commerce Boom." *Huffington Post,* October 2, 2014. http://www.huffingtonpost.com/shehzad-h-qazi/chinas-new-open-door-the-b_5917728.html.

Roebuck, Martin. "Onward and Upward for UPS in Europe as It Eyes 3-D Printing as the 'Next Big Thing.'" *Loadstar,* September 29, 2014. http://theloadstar.co.uk/upsin3d/.

Rusch, Ed. "Using Social Media in the Supply Chain." *Manufacturing Business Technology,* August 6, 2014. http://www.mbtmag.com/articles/2014/08/using-social-media-supply-chain.

Shepherd, Ben. "Logistics Costs and Competitiveness: Measurement and Trade Policy Applications." Washington, DC: World Bank, 2011.
http://siteresources.worldbank.org/INTTRANSPORT/Resources/336291-1239112757744/5997693-1294344242332/Logistics_costs.pdf.

Stasinakis, Argyris. "Logistics Providers Can See the Big Picture (Thanks to an App) As AIS Comes of Age." *Loadstar,* August 20, 2014. http://theloadstar.co.uk/ais/.

Supply Chain Matters. "The UPS Store Expands 3D Printing across the U.S.A." *SupplyChain247,* October 1, 2014.
http://www.supplychain247.com/article/the_ups_store_expands_3d_printing_across_the_usa.

———. "Trends That Will Shape the Supply Chain in 2014." *SupplyChain247,* January 28, 2014.
http://www.supplychain247.com/article/trends_that_will_shape_the_supply_chain_in_2014/one_network_enterprises.

Szakonyi, Mark. "Asia's Big Logistics Picture." *Journal of Commerce* 15, no. 22 (October 27, 2014).

Transport Intelligence. "Stifel Logistics Confidence Index October 2014," October 16, 2014. http://www.transportintelligence.com/stifel-index/articles-and-papers/.

U.S. Department of Commerce (USDOC). Bureau of Economic Analysis (BEA). *Survey of Current Business*, October 2014, table 3.2.

———. International Data, Interactive tables: "Table 3.1: Services Supplied to Foreign Persons by U.S. MNEs through Their MOFAs, by Industry of Affiliate and by Country of Affiliate," and "Table 4.1: Services Supplied to U.S. Persons by Foreign MNEs through Their MOUSA, by Industry of Affiliate and by Country of UBO," October 24, 2014. http://www.bea.gov/iTable/iTable.cfm?ReqID=62&step=1#reqid=62&step=6&isuri=1&6221=0&6220=1,2,3,4,5&6210=4&6200=236&6224=&6223=&6222=53,54,56,57&6230=1.

U.S. International Trade Commission (USITC). *Logistics Services: An Overview of the Global Market and Potential Effects of Removing Trade Impediments*. USITC Publication 3770. Washington, DC: USITC, May 2005. http://www.usitc.gov/publications/332/pub3770.pdf.

———. *Digital Trade in the U.S. and Global Economies, Part 1*. USITC Publication 4415. Washington, DC: USITC, July 2013. http://www.usitc.gov/publications/332/pub4415.pdf.

———. *Digital Trade in the U.S. and Global Economies, Part 2*. USITC Publication 4485. Washington, DC: USITC, August 2014. http://www.usitc.gov/publications/332/pub4485.pdf.

Van Leeuwen, Thomas. "1PL to 5PL: The Differences between a 3PL Logistics Provider and Other Logistics Service Providers," June 17, 2014. http://logistics.bcr.com.au/blog/1pl-to-5pl-the-differences-between-a-3pl-logistics-provider-and-other-logistics-service-providers.

World Trade Organization (WTO). *World Trade Report 2014*. http://www.wto.org/english/res_e/publications_e/wtr14_e.htm.

———. Time Series on International Trade. http://stat.wto.org/StatisticalProgram/WSDBViewData.aspx?Language=E (accessed December 11, 2014).

Yusof, Shukor, and Pey Herng Yap. "Global Industry Surveys: Airlines; Asia." *Standard & Poor's*, January 2014.

Chapter 4
Maritime Transport Services

Summary

The maritime transport services industry, which includes firms that provide both shipping and port services, is as an important facilitator of global merchandise trade. In 2013, total revenues of the top 10 global container shipping firms reached $110.0 billion, a decrease of 4.7 percent from the previous year, compared to annual growth of 0.9 percent during 2008–12. Overall, maritime firms are deeply vulnerable to economic downturns that dampen consumer demand and ultimately decrease the volume of cross-border trade in goods. Following the global recession of 2008–09,[150] large container shipping firms enhanced their efforts to become cost-competitive. These efforts included investing in larger, more fuel-efficient ships and participating in global alliances, allowing firms to share resources and spread operating costs. The container shipping segment of the maritime transport services industry is now both highly consolidated and highly globalized, having been also affected by a wave of international mergers and acquisitions among the largest firms beginning in the late 1990s.

Port services providers, including a growing number of private entitities, are also becoming globalized. Firms like Hong Kong's Hutchinson Port Holdings and Singapore's PSA International manage in excess of 50 port terminals worldwide. Port reform began in developed countries in the 1980s and has since taken hold in several developing countries, including countries in Africa, Asia, and Latin America. In developing countries, port reform has emphasized expanding port infrastructure and improving port productivity to accommodate the countries' growing participation in global supply chains.

In 2013, the United States posted a cross-border trade deficit in maritime transport services of $19.1 billion, nearly double the deficit recorded in 2009 ($9.6 billion). The U.S. deficit reflects a larger trend in merchandise trade in which U.S. imports exceeded U.S. exports by 48 percent in 2013. During that year, the top five U.S. export and import markets for maritime transport services remained unchanged from 2012 and included Japan, Taiwan, Germany, the Republic of Korea (South Korea), and China. At the same time, total sales for foreign affiliates of U.S. maritime transport services firms reached $8.7 billion in 2012, the latest year for which such data are available. This was slightly higher than sales by U.S. affiliates of foreign maritime transport services firms, which totaled $6.5 billion.

---

[150] OECD, Quarterly National Accounts database, n.d. (accessed February 12, 2015).

Introduction

Maritime transport services are one of four primary transport modes, which also include air, road, and rail transport services.[151] These four modes often complement one another in the movement of goods through increasingly vast and complex global transportation networks. Maritime transport is closely linked to merchandise trade, and it has historically accounted for the largest share of the international transport of goods. On average, roughly 80 percent of the volume of global merchandise trade (i.e., the sum of both exports and imports) is transported by water; in countries such as China, 90 percent of international merchandise trade is conveyed through maritime transport.[152]

The maritime transport services industry supplies a broad range of activities. These include water transportation services; supporting services for water transport, such as port and waterway operation services; and cargo handling, storage, and warehousing services. Water transportation services involve the transport of passengers or freight on maritime vessels that travel between coastal or deep-sea ports, between these ports and the U.S. and Canadian Great Lakes, and within inland lakes and waterways.[153] Port and waterway operation services include, among other things, the operation of marine and passenger terminal facilities, and the servicing of locks and canals.[154] Cargo-handling service, and storage and warehousing services include the loading, unloading, and storage of maritime cargo. These services are provided to vessels by a port operator using the port's own labor, equipment, and facilities, in the case of an "operating" port. Alternatively, they are provided using the labor, equipment, and facilities of concessionaires or private-sector operators in the case of a "landlord" port.[155]

The geographic distribution of seaborne trade has shifted over the past few decades, so that developing, rather than developed, countries now account for the majority of maritime import volume. The increase in developing countries' share of import cargo has been stimulated by the expanding role that these economies play in global value chains and by their growing middle class.[156] To illustrate, in 1970, developing countries' share of maritime import cargo was 18 percent; by 2013, this share had more than tripled to 60 percent.[157] During the same period,

---

[151] Pipeline transport is not included. Air freight transport is discussed in chapter 3, "Logistics Services."

[152] UNCTAD, *Review of Maritime Transport 2013*, 2013, xi; Dupin, "China Seeks Boost to Shipping Industry," September 4, 2014.

[153] This chapter does not discuss maritime passenger transport services.

[154] Other supporting services for water transport include piloting and tugboat assistance services (where vessels are guided into or out of harbors), navigation aid services, and vessel salvage and refloating services.

[155] UN, *Provisional Central Product Classification, 1991*, 213–20. See box 4.1 for a discussion of the port sector.

[156] UNCTAD, *Review of Maritime Transport 2012*, 2012, 6 and 11.

[157] The UN categorizes countries as "developing" or "developed" for statistical purposes, and the lists of such countries may change over time.

developing countries' share of export cargo remained high throughout: they accounted for 63 percent of cargo loaded onto maritime vessels for international transport in 1970 and 61 percent of such cargo in 2013.[158] Changing global production patterns have also begun to alter the locus of maritime trade. While East-West trade between Asia and Europe/North America continues to predominate, intraregional and "South-South" trade are growing, particularly among developing countries in Africa, Asia, and Latin America.[159]

Market Conditions in Global Maritime Transport Services

In 2013, the five countries with the largest shipping fleets were Greece, Japan, China, Germany, and South Korea (table 4.1).[160] Together, these five countries accounted for 53 percent of

Table 4.1: Top 10 countries with the largest maritime fleets as of January 1, 2014

Rank[a]	Country	Fleet size (million dwt)	Share of world maritime tonnage (percentage)	Total number of vessels	National flag (percentage of dwt)	Foreign flag (percentage of dwt)
1	Greece	258	15.4	3,825	17	73
2	Japan	229	13.6	4,022	8	92
3	China	200	11.9	5,405	37	63
4	Germany	127	7.6	3,699	13	87
5	South Korea	78	4.7	1,568	11	79
6	Singapore	74	4.4	2,120	55	45
7	United States	57	3.4	1,927	15	85
8	United Kingdom	53	3.2	1,233	16	84
9	Taiwan	47	2.8	862	8	92
10	Norway	43	2.6	1,864	16	94
World total		1,677		47,601		

Source: UNCTAD, *Review of Maritime Transport 2014,* 2014, 33–37, table 2.3: "Ownership of the World Fleet, as of 1 January 2014 (dwt)."

[a] Rank based on total tonnage of fleet.

---

[158] UNCTAD, *Review of Maritime Transport 2014,* 2014, 7, figure 1.3(b), "Participation of Developing Economies in World Seaborne Trade, Selected Years (percentage share in world tonnage)."

[159] UNCTAD, *Review of Maritime Transport 2013,* 2013, 3; Leonel "South-South Trade—Rewiring the Global Economy," n.d. (accessed September 10, 2014); Hapag-Lloyd, Annual Report 2013, 2013, 67; World Shipping Council, "Trade Routes (TEU Shipped), 2012." "South-South" trade refers to trade between developing countries.

[160] UNCTAD, *Review of Maritime Transport 2014,* 2014, 39, figure 2.5, "Top 20 Shipowning Nations, Beneficial Ownership, 1 January 2014 (1,000 dwt by country/economy of ownership)." Beneficial ownership refers to the country in which the company that has the primary commercial interest in the ship is located. In many cases, the country of beneficial ownership is separate from the country where the ship is registered.

global maritime capacity.[161] The United States ranked seventh, behind Singapore, in terms of the size of its maritime fleet.[162] Developing countries ranked among the top 20 countries by fleet size, although their share of global maritime capacity was considerably smaller than that of developed countries. For example, in 2013, Turkey's maritime fleet accounted for roughly 1.7 percent of global maritime capacity and ranked number 12 worldwide, while India ranked 16th, less than 1.3 percent of global maritime tonnage.[163] In general, the largest growth in fleet size has been among countries with open registries, such as Panama and Liberia.[164] This reflects the widespread practice among ship owners of registering their vessels in countries with less stringent regulatory environments and lower labor and operating costs.[165]

The largest global shipping firms do not reflect, in some cases, the countries with the largest maritime fleets. In 2013, the top five container shipping lines were Mediterranean Shipping Co. (MSC) (Switzerland), Maersk Line (Denmark), CMA CGM Group (France), Evergreen Line (Taiwan), and China Ocean Shipping Company (COSCO) (table 4.2).[166] They were followed by Hapag-Lloyd Group (Germany), China Shipping Lines Container Co., Ltd. (CSCL), Hanjin Shipping

---

[161] UNCTAD, *Review of Maritime Transport 2014,* 2014, 37, figure 2.3, "Ownership of the World Fleet, as of 1 January 2014 (dwt)." Fleet size is calculated as the total volume of deadweight tons (dwt) that all the ships in a country's fleet comprise, rather than the number of ships in that fleet. However, there is a large, though not exact, correspondence between the number of ships in a country's fleet and its total cargo-carrying capacity.

[162] UNCTAD, *Review of Maritime Transport 2014,* 2014, 39, figure 2.5, "Top 20 Shipowning Nations, Beneficial Ownership, 1 January 2014 (1,000 dwt by country/economy of ownership)."

[163] UNCTAD, *Review of Maritime Transport 2014,* 2014, 33–37, 39, figure 2.3, "Ownership of the World Fleet, as of 1 January 2014 (dwt)," and figure 2.5, "Top 20 Shipowning Nations, Beneficial Ownership, 1 January 2014 (1,000 dwt by country/economy of ownership)."

[164] A country with an open registry permits vessels from other countries to be registered under it and fly its national flag. As noted, countries with open registries do not own many of the vessels in their own fleets. For example, both Panama and Liberia own less than 1 percent of the vessels that are recorded in their shipping registries. At present, roughly two-thirds of the global maritime fleet (by tonnage) is registered under so-called "flags of convenience," or open registries. UNCTAD, *Review of Maritime Transport 2014,* 2014, 44, table 2.5, "The 35 Flags of Registration with the Largest Registered Fleets, as of 1 January 2014 (dwt); Rodrigue, "Maritime Transportation: Drivers for the Shipping and Port Industries," 2010, 7.

[165] OECD, "Regulatory Issues in International Maritime Transport," 2001, 14–15.

[166] UNCTAD, *Review of Maritime Transport 2014,* 2014, 40, table 2.4, "The 50 Leading Liner Companies, 1 January 2014 (number of ships and total shipboard capacity deployed, in TEUs, ranked by TEU)." Container ships carry packaged cargo in cellular units that can be offloaded onto railcars or tractor-trailers and transported to their final destination. A standard container measures 20 feet long by 8 feet wide and is referred to as a twenty-foot equivalent unit (TEU). In general, maritime vessels may be categorized by class (e.g., container ship, tanker, dry bulk, roll-on/roll-off); the type of cargo they transport (e.g., bulk, general, liquid, or container); their weight (typically expressed in deadweight tons, or dwt); and where they are deployed—for example, in the deep sea and along the coast (oceangoing vessels), or within the Great Lakes and inland waterways). Liner shipping is the transport of goods in large-capacity ocean liners (principally container ships and roll on/roll off vessels) that travel on regular schedules over fixed routes. World Shipping Council, "Glossary of Industry Terms," n.d. (accessed October 3, 2014).

Company Limited (South Korea), APL Limited (Singapore),[167] and United Arab Shipping Company (S.A.G.) (Dubai, United Arab Emirates (UAE)). Collectively, these 10 companies accounted for a 60 percent share of global container carrying capacity in 2013.[168] The total revenue of the 10 leading container shipping lines was slightly more than $110 billion in 2013, the latest year for which such data are available. This represents a 4.7 percent decrease from the previous year—a departure from the average annual growth of 0.9 percent during the 2008–12 period. Overall, profitability in the global container shipping industry is elusive. This is due to the deeply commoditized nature of the container shipping business (in which freight rates fluctuate rapidly with changes in supply and demand), as well as its high capital costs.[169] The global recession of 2008–09 exacerbated the financial challenges faced by the shipping industry and is evident in the negative to modest revenue growth experienced by most of the top-10 firms within the past five years.[170]

Table 4.2: Top 10 global container shipping firms, 2013

Rank[a]	Company	Country of headquarters	Share of global container ship capacity (percentage of TEUs)	Revenue ($million)[b]	2012 Revenue ($millions)[b]	Average annual growth in revenue (percent), 2008–12	2013 revenue ($millions)[b]	Percentage change in revenue, 2012–13
1	MSC	Switzerland	13.1	c	c	c	c	c
2	Maersk Line	Denmark	12.6	52,901	48,601	(2.1)	45,124	(7.2)
3	CMA CGM Group	France	7.6	15,100	15,923	1.3	15,902	(0.1)
4	Evergreen Line	Taiwan	5.5	[d]2,050	4,843	24.0	4,637	(4.3)
5	COSCO Container Lines Limited	China	4.4	[d]6,886	11,407	13.4	10,132	(11.2)
6	Hapag-Lloyd Group	Germany	3.8	9,181	8,632	(1.5)	8,283	(4.0)

[167] APL was formerly known as American President Lines, a U.S. company headquartered in Oakland, California. APL was purchased by Singaporean maritime firm Neptune Orient Lines (NOL) in 1997 and became its wholly owned subsidiary. The APL brand name is used for NOL's container shipping business. NOL company website, "Our Brands," n.d., http://www.nol.com.sg/wps/portal/nol (accessed February 18, 2015); USITC, *Recent Trends in U.S. Services Trade: 2000*, 2000, 17-4.

[168] UNCTAD, *Review of Maritime Transport 2014*, 40–41, table 2.4, "The 50 Leading Liner Companies, 1 January 2014 (number of ships and total shipboard capacity deployed, in TEUs, ranked by TEU)." In 2012, container ships transported 52 percent of global cargo by value, as compared to tankers (22 percent), general cargo vessels (20 percent), and dry bulk carriers (6 percent). UNCTAD, *Review of Maritime Transport 2013*, 61.

[169] Capital costs are highest for ship leasing, ship repair and maintenance, and the purchase of fuel.

[170] Neptune Orient Lines Limited, *Annual Report 2013*, 2013, 2.

Rank[a]	Company	Country of headquarters	Share of global container ship capacity (percentage of TEUs)	Revenue ($million)[b]	2012 Revenue ($millions)[b]	Average annual growth in revenue (percent), 2008–12	2013 revenue ($millions)[b]	Percentage change in revenue, 2012–13
7	CSCL	China	3.7	5,662	5,303	(1.6)	5,525	4.2
8	Hanjin Shipping Company Limited	Korea	3.4	9,312	9,571	0.7	9,719	1.5
9	APL Limited	Singapore	3.2	9,285	9,512	(0.6)	8,831	(7.2)
10	United Arab Shipping Company	Dubai, UAE	3.1	1,853	2,498	7.8	2,667	6.8
Total				112,230	116,290	0.9	110,820	(4.7)

Source: Compiled by USITC from UNCTAD, *Review of Maritime Transport 2014*, 2014, 40–41, table 2.4, "The 50 Leading Liner Companies, 1 January 2014 (number of ships and total shipboard capacity deployed, in TEUs, ranked by TEU)"; Steelguru.com, "Hagag Lloyd Operating Profit Up by 19 Percent YoY," March 27, 2009; 3PL News, "After a Year Shaped by Global Crisis," May 4, 2010; Hanjin Shipping, "Hanjin Shipping Holdings Company Limited" (accessed September 26, 2014); and Bureau Van Dijk, ORBIS Database, "United Arab Shipping Company (S.A.G.)" (accessed November 25, 2014). Currency conversion at Yahoo Finance, http://finance.yahoo.com/currency-converter (accessed September 30, 2014, and October 1, 2014).

[a] Rank is based on share of global container ship capacity as measured in twenty-foot equivalent units (TEUs), or the cargo-carrying capacity of a standard shipping container that is 20 feet long and 8 feet wide.

[b] Revenue figures include those for the parent firm of the container shipping line and its subsidiaries, including its container shipping business.

[c] No information available.

[d] Estimated based on data from Hoover's, "China COSCO Holdings Company," n.d. (accessed October 1, 2014), and Hoover's, "Evergreen Marine Corporation (Taiwan)," n.d. (accessed October 1, 2014).

Mergers and Acquisitions Have Been Prevalent among Large Container Shipping Firms

The composition of the top 10 global shipping firms has altered recently, continuing a pattern of change that has extended over the past two decades, as companies have either merged with or acquired other large maritime firms in order to combine shipping assets and extend transit routes. For example, in 1996, French state-owned Compagnie Générale Maritime (CGM) was privatized and purchased by the privately held Compagnie Maritime d'Affrètement (CMA) to form the CMA CGM Group. CMA CGM acquired French shipping firm Delmas in 2006, becoming the third largest container shipping firm in the world.[171] Likewise, Maersk expanded its fleet and route network through the purchase of U.S. container shipping firm SeaLand in 1999. The purchase allowed Maersk to acquire an additional 70 container ships, as well as to provide

---

[171] As measured by container capacity, not revenues. Motorship, "CMA CGM Acquires Delmas," September 13, 2005.

shipping services in the U.S. domestic maritime (cabotage) market.[172] In 2004, Maersk also acquired container shipping firm P&O Nedlloyd, itself the result of a 1997 merger between British maritime firm P&O Group and Dutch container shipping line Royal Nedlloyd.[173] Finally, in 2005, German-based Hapag-Lloyd purchased British-Canadian container shipping firm CP Ships, extending Hapag-Lloyd's Asia-Pacific regional coverage.[174] More recently, in September 2014, Hapag-Lloyd received EU antitrust approval to merge with Chilean container line Compañia Sudamericana de Vapores (CSAV). The merger will allow Hapag-Lloyd to offer additional service between Europe and Latin America, and to rise from the sixth- to the fourth- largest container shipping firm in the world.[175]

Many of the major shipping firms manage a portfolio of maritime-related businesses that complement their container shipping operations and, in some cases, help them mitigate financial risks from a potential decrease in container shipping demand. Maersk, the largest and perhaps most diversified global shipping firm, has three primary business lines besides container shipping (Maersk Line): port operation (APM Terminals),[176] oil and gas services (Maersk Oil), and offshore services (Maersk Drilling and Services). It also has separate subsidiaries devoted to logistics services and vessel salvage and supply services.[177] Like Maersk, Singapore-based Neptune Orient Lines (NOL) includes in its portfolio one of the largest third-party global logistics service providers, APL Logistics. APL accounted for nearly 20 percent of NOL's revenues in 2013.[178] Shipping lines COSCO, Evergreen, and Hanjin each has a subsidiary that manages port terminal operations.[179] In addition, COSCO maintains separate container

---

[172] The United States no longer has a presence among the top 20 global container shipping lines. See discussion of maritime services in USITC, *Recent Trends in U.S. Services Trade: 2000,* 2000, 17-3, 17-4. However, the Jones Act requires that the transport of oceanbone cargo between U.S. ports be provided on vessels that are built in the United States, and that are owned and operated by U.S. citizens. The Jones Act is the shorthand name given to section 27 of the 1920 Merchant Marine Act (46 U.S.C. 883).

[173] FIS.com, "P&O Nedlloyd Company Headquarters," n.d. (accessed September 16, 2014).

[174] Hapag-Lloyd, "CP Ships Finalizes Plans," December 27, 2005.

[175] As measured by container capacity, not revenues. Leach, "EU Approves Merger of Hapag-Lloyd, CSAV," September 11, 2014; CSAV, "European Commission Approves Merger" (accessed September 19, 2014).

[176] Private sector operators typically manage the "superstructure" of a port, which includes the cranes, forklifts, and other equipment associated with cargo handling. WTO, Secretariat, "Maritime Transport Services: Background Note," June 7, 2010, 31.

[177] A.P. Moller-Maersk A/S, *Annual Report 2013,* 2013, 3–4.

[178] Neptune Orient Lines Limited, *Annual Report 2013,* 2013, 1, 7, and 11. NOL Group is the holding company for APL (container shipping) and APL Logistics.

[179] China COSCO Holdings Company Limited, *Annual Report 2013,* 2013, 14; Evergreen Marine Corp. (Taiwan) Ltd., *2013 Annual Report,* 2013, 35; Hanjin Shipping, *2011 Business Report,* December 31, 2011, 7. COSCO is partly owned by the Chinese government.

leasing and ship repair businesses, while Hanjin operates a subsidiary that supplies bulk (non-containerized) shipping services.[180]

The Port Services Industry Has Evolved Rapidly over the Past Few Decades

The port services sector is inextricably linked to maritime shipping, and firms within this industry comprise a mixture of global shipping lines, government entities, and private sector operators. As mentioned, 4 of the top 10 global shipping firms—Maersk, COSCO, Evergreen, and Hanjin—are also among the top 10 port terminal operators (table 4.3). Of the remaining top 10 port terminal operators, the largest and most globalized are PSA International, Hutchinson Port Holdings (HPH), and DP World.[181] These firms were formed through a combination of corporatization, merger and acquisition, and global network expansion, much of which occurred during a wider trend towards port reform in the 1980s and 1990s (box 4.1).[182]

Table 4.3: Top 10 global port operators, 2012

Rank	Name of port operator	Country of headquarters	Throughput (million TEUs)	Share of global throughput (percentage)
1	PSA International	Singapore	50.9	8.2
2	Hutchinson Port Holdings (HPH)	Hong Kong, China	44.8	7.2
3	APM Terminals	Singapore	33.7	5.4
4	DP World	Dubai (UAE)	33.4	5.4
5	COSCO Group	China	17.0	2.7
6	Terminal Investment Limited (TIL)	Netherlands	13.5	2.2
7	China Shipping Terminal Development	China	8.6	1.4
8	Hanjin	Korea	7.8	1.3
9	Evergreen	Taiwan	7.5	1.2
10	Eurogate	Germany	6.5	1.0

Source: Drewry, "Drewry's Top Ten Global Terminal Operators," August 27, 2013.

PSA International (Singapore) was originally established as the state-affiliated Port of Singapore Authority, responsible for the development, operation, and regulation of Singapore's ports.

---

[180] China COSCO Holdings, *Annual Report 2013*, 14; Hanjin Shipping, "Bulk Vessel Fleet," n.d. (accessed October 3, 2014).

[181] Rodrigue and Notteboom, "Global Networks in the Container Terminal Operating Industry," Spring 2011, 13–14.

[182] Rodrigue and Notteboom, "Global Networks in the Container Terminal Operating Industry," Spring 2011, 13–14. Under *corporatization,* a publicly owned port authority retains ownership of the physical infrastructure of a port, but the port's commercial activities (e.g., cargo handling) are performed by private firms. Under this scenario, the port authority operates as a corporation, with the private sector terminal operators serving as its subsidiaries. By contrast, under *privatization,* publicly owned port assets are sold to private sector entities. Everett and Robinson, "Chapter 12, Port Reform: The Australian Experience," 2007, 264.

Box 4.1: A snapshot of maritime port reform

Starting in the 1980s, several countries began reforming their maritime port sectors by permitting private-sector companies to operate some or all of their port terminal facilities. Prior to reform, most ports were "public service," or "operating" ports in which a state or local port authority owns the land, facilities, and equipment at the port and is responsible for providing port services.[a] After the reforms began, many ports transitioned to the "landlord" model, whereby the port authority still owns the physical infrastructure of the port but permits private sector firms, often through concession agreements, to supply port services.[b] In addition, some countries pursued wider reform efforts by joining in public-private partnerships (PPPs) to develop port infrastructure or, alternatively, through the outright sale of port assets to private entities (privatization).[c]

Early examples of port reform occurred in Thailand where, in 1989, the government signed an agreement with a shipping line to manage the country's new port terminals in Phuket and Songhla; and in Argentina, where in 1992, the government offered 25-year concessions to private firms for the management of the country's six port terminals in Buenos Aires. During the same time, port authorities in both Hong Kong and the Philippines used build-operate-transfer (BOT) agreements to partner with private companies to expand port terminal facilities.[d] Separate and more extensive reforms were undertaken in the United Kingdom in 1983, when the government-owned port authority was privatized through the sale of equity shares, becoming a private entity, Associated British Ports (ABP).[e]

The corporatization of ports commenced in the early 1990s. Australia was among the first countries to begin this process, along with Hong Kong, Singapore, and the UAE.[f] Through corporatization, a statutory port authority is transformed, by law, into a government-owned corporation. Private firms provide most commercial activities, such as cargo handling, and manage individual port terminals. Under this model, private rather than public resources are used to build, expand, and manage port terminals. Corporatization also encourages market-based competition among ports which, in turn, may increase the sector's efficiency and productivity.[g]

Corporatization has resulted in the emergence of global terminal operators, either large container shipping lines or private port management firms that operate a growing network of port terminals. Already noted examples include shipping lines Maersk and COSCO, as well as port terminal operators DP World, HPH, and PSA International.[h] Increasing participation in the port sector by financial institutions is also an important trend and has continued in earnest since the 1990s. Such equity investments offer potential gains to financial entities while funding the development of port networks. Port terminal operators ABP, DP World, HPH, and PSA International all are financed through private equity funds.[i]

[a] Kent, "Port Reform, Privatization, and Regulation," December 17, 2008, 10.

[b] A concession is a long-term agreement that permits a private firm to provide commercial services at a port using the firm's own equipment. In exchange for use of the land at the port, the private firm agrees to pay rent to the port authority as well as to invest in the building, renovation, or expansion of the port's terminal(s). Rodrigue, "The Geography of Transport Systems," n.d. (accessed November 5, 2015).

[c] Turpin, "PPP in Ports, Landlord Port Model," April 12, 2013, 8.

[d] Haarmeyer and Yorke, "Port Privatization: An International Perspective," April 1993, 8–9.

[e] Haarmeyer and Yorke, "Port Privatization: An International Perspective," April 1993, 10–11; UNCTAD, *Review of Maritime Transport 2007*, 2007, 87.

[f] Everett and Robinson, "Port Reform: The Australian Experience," 2007, 262.

[g] Everett and Robinson, "Port Reform: The Australian Experience," 2007, 262; Rodrigue, "The Geography of Transport Systems," n.d. (accessed November 5, 2014). Although 80 percent of global container volume is handled by private port terminal operators, this trend is not evident in Africa, where between 50 and 70 percent of container cargo is processed by public sector port entities. African Development Bank, "Reforms and the Regulatory Framework of African Ports," 2010, 78.

[h] Turpin, "PPP in Ports, Landlord Port Model," April 12, 2013, 27.

[i] UNCTAD, *Review of Maritime Transport 2007*, 2007, 87; Moody's Investor Services, "Privately Managed Port Companies," May 13, 2013, 4.

In 1996, PSA transferred its regulatory functions to the Maritime and Port Authority of Singapore and formed PSA Corporation Limited to oversee the port operations business. During the same year, PSA Corporation Limited entered into a joint venture with the Chinese government to manage the port of Dalian, China.[183] The company has since extended its global footprint to an additional 14 countries and now manages ports in Belgium, India, Japan, and Saudi Arabia, among others.[184]

Unlike PSA International, HPH was founded as a private company. It is the subsidiary of a global port investment firm based in Hong Kong, Hutchinson Whampoa Limited. HPH operates 52 ports in 26 countries and, in 2006, sold a 20 percent equity stake in its port business to PSA International.[185]

DP World was originally established as the Dubai Ports Authority, with jurisdiction over ports in the UAE. The entity was corporatized in 1999 and, through its acquisition of U.S. firm CSX World Terminals in 2005, and the terminal operations of UK shipping firm Peninsular & Oriental Steam Navigation (P&O) Company in 2006, became the fourth-largest port terminal operator in the world.[186] DP World currently manages a portfolio of 65 port terminals, including terminals in Africa, Europe, India, and the Middle East.[187]

Maritime Transport Services Remain Highly Regulated

The maritime industry is subject to myriad regulations, some of which may affect foreign firms' ability to provide—or access—shipping and port services. In general, maritime shipping service providers are required to comply with broad international regulations that concern the safety of vessels and crew, and the prevention of pollution from ships. These regulations are

---

[183] PSA company website, "Ports of Call," n.d., http://www.internationalpsa.com/about/mission.html (accessed September 25, 2014); *Online Asia Times,* "A New Era in Asian Shipping," September 2, 2000.

[184] PSA company website, "Ports of Call," n.d., http://www.internationalpsa.com/about/mission.html (accessed September 25, 2014); PSA, "Our Business," n.d. (accessed February 13, 2015). In 2003, PSA International PTE Ltd. became the holding company for PSA Corporation. PSA International is wholly owned by Singapore-based investment firm Temasek Holdings, which, in turn, is owned by the government of Singapore. Moody's, "Rating Action: Moody's Affirms PSA International," October 17, 2013.

[185] Hutchinson Port Holdings, "Company Profile," n.d. (accessed September 25, 2014); *Economic Times,* "Hutchinson Sells 20% Port Stake to Rival," April 22, 2006.

[186] DP World, *Annual Report and Accounts,* 2013, 2013, 6. DP World is wholly owned by the government of Dubai through a holding company. Kane, "DP World Demands S&P Withdraw Credit Rating," May 18, 2012.

[187] DP World, "Our Business," n.d. (accessed September 29, 2014).

established under the United Nations' International Maritime Organization (IMO) and apply to nearly all OECD members.[188] Like environmental and safety laws, regulations pertaining to maritime cargo security are applied internationally and have been developed under the auspices of both the IMO and the World Customs Organization (WCO).[189] Maritime firms are also subject to national laws that regulate commercial activity in the sector, such as the participation of foreign firms in domestic shipping and port operations (box 4.2). For example, many countries maintain cabotage laws that restrict foreign-flagged vessels from transporting cargo between a country's coastal ports and within its domestic lakes and waterways.[190] Likewise, certain national laws limit foreign investment in port operations and/or require that foreign shipping firms use the services and equipment of state-owned port authorities for cargo handling.[191]

Box 4.2: Types of barriers to trade in maritime transport services

Entry, or market access barriers (GATS mode 1):

- Cargo preference (a.k.a. cargo reservation) mechanisms.[a]

- Cargo sharing arrangements[b] (via bilateral and multilateral agreements between trading partners).

- Participation in liner conferences[c] in which shipping firms collectively agree on service schedules and freight rates.

Establishment, or commercial presence barriers (GATS mode 3):

- Ship registration or flagging restrictions[d] that include nationality requirements on vessel ownership.

- Limitations on foreign investment in government-owned shipping lines.

- Limitations on foreign investment in domestic port operations.

- Requirements to operate through domestic shipping agents.

Operational barriers (GATS modes 1 and 3):

---

[188] See, for example, OECD, "Regulatory Issues in International Maritime Transport," 2001, annex D, "Major Safety and Environmental Regulations," 97–103.

[189] WTO, Secretariat, "Maritime Transport Services: Background Note," June 7, 2010, 2; Peterson and Treat, "The Post 9/11 Framework for Cargo Security," September 2009, 1–30. Labor regulations that pertain to both ship crew and port workers are also significant.

[190] Cabotage refers to the ability of foreign-owned ships to provide domestic maritime transport service.

[191] WTO, Secretariat, "Maritime Transport Services: Background Note," June 7, 2010, 31.

- Requirements to use domestic firms for port service operations (i.e., pilotage, towing, tug assistance, navigation, berthing, waste disposal, anchorage, and casting off).

- Requirements to use domestic firms for ancillary services at ports (i.e., cargo-handling, storage and warehousing services, and container station and depot services).

- Requirements to use domestic firms for other auxiliary transport services (i.e., customs brokerage and freight forwarding).

- Cabotage restrictions.

Barriers to the movement of natural persons (GATS mode 4):

- Domestic crewing requirements for vessels providing cabotage.

- Limitations on the temporary movement of executives, senior managers, and/or specialists.

Source: Adapted from McGuire, Schuele, and Smith, "Restrictiveness of International Trade in Maritime Services," 2000, 176–78. See also the World Bank's Services Trade Restrictions Database for a listing of mode 1 and mode 3 maritime transport restrictions by country at http://iresearch.worldbank.org/services.trade/home.htm.

[a] Cargo preference refers to a country's reserving to national vessels the right to carry export and import cargo. For example, certain countries, such as the United States, reserve the transport of government-owned cargo for vessels in the U.S. merchant fleet.

[b] Cargo-sharing arrangements occur when parties to bilateral or multilateral agreements allocate national cargoes to the vessels of signatory countries.

[c] A liner conference refers to an international group of ocean carriers that agree to establish shipping rates and service schedules on the trade routes that they serve. Liner conferences or "conference agreements" fall into one of two distinct categories of cooperative arrangements between ocean carriers. These two categories are pricing agreements and operational agreements. Pricing agreements include conference agreements and "rate discussion agreements" (RDAs) that establish common freight rates and carrier practices among their members. For the most part, conference agreements are seldom deployed by U.S. liner vessels, having been replaced by RDAs. Separately, operational agreements include vessel-sharing agreements, joint service agreements, cooperative working agreements (CWAs), and "non-rate discussion agreements without rate authority." FMC, *50th Annual Report*, Fiscal Year 2011, 109–11.

[d] Ship registration requirements limit vessels that are permitted to fly a country's flag to those owned and operated by nationals of the country. Typically, ships that are registered in a particular country enjoy favorable tax treatment, are permitted to provide cabotage services, and may participate in cargo preference programs. By contrast, countries that have a liberal registration regime (i.e., where nationality is not a precondition for registration), such as Panama and Liberia, are identified as "flags of convenience."

Efforts to reduce barriers to trade in maritime shipping and port services have seen limited progress to date. In particular, a collective agreement liberalizing maritime transport services was not reached at the conclusion of the Uruguay Round of trade negotiations under the WTO's

General Agreement on Trade in Services (GATS).[192] Nonetheless, at present, 76 WTO members have scheduled commitments on maritime transport services (excluding cabotage) and auxiliary services, such as cargo-handling services and warehousing and storage services.[193] Apart from the WTO, some countries have undertaken bilateral and multilateral efforts to liberalize trade in maritime transport services. For instance, the United States signed maritime agreements with China and Brazil in 2003 and 2005, respectively, to improve access to each other's maritime markets.[194] Similarly, in 2007, a maritime agreement was signed between the members of the Association of Southeast Asian Nations (ASEAN) and China aimed at increasing the efficiency of maritime transport services among signatory countries.[195]

Emerging Demand and Supply Factors

In recent years, the demand for and supply of maritime transport services have been influenced by several factors. On the demand side, the most significant of these is rising developing-country participation in merchandise trade and global supply chains. On the supply side, the major factors are the increasing deployment of large container ships and a growing trend toward global shipping alliances.

Developing Countries´ Demand for Maritime Transport Services Is Increasing

Developing countries' participation in merchandise trade has grown considerably over the years and, with that, their demand for maritime services. In 2011, developing countries accounted for more than $17.0 trillion in global merchandise exports and imports, compared to $19.0 trillion

---

[192] The WTO's Negotiating Group on Maritime Services commenced negotiations during the Uruguay Round. The objective of the group was to liberalize maritime transport services using a "three pillar" approach. This approach focused on the following core areas for negotiation: maritime transport services; maritime auxiliary services; and port services. The group failed to reach a collective agreement and ceased negotiations in June 1996. In 2001, with a view to resuming maritime services discussions, Australia proposed adding a fourth pillar, "multimodal" services. Multimodal services refer to the integration of two or more forms of transport, and can include access to trucking, rail, and inland waterway transport services. (UNCTAD defines multimodal services as the door-to-door transport of goods under the supervision of a single transport operator.) Because multimodal services include a range of transportation services, some members of the group suggested that negotiating such services would exceed the intended scope of maritime negotiations under the GATS.

[193] WTO, I-TIP Services Database, n.d. (accessed October 8, 2014). The European Union is counted as one country.

[194] HKTDC, "US, China Sign Historic Maritime Agreement," December 24, 2003; USDOT, MARAD, "Agreement on Maritime Transport," September 30, 2005.

[195] ASEAN, "2007 Agreement on Maritime Transport," November 2, 2007. The 10 member countries of ASEAN are Brunei Darussalam, Cambodia, Indonesia, Laos, Malaysia, Myanmar, the Philippines, Singapore, Thailand, and Vietnam.

for developed countries.[196] Merchandise trade with developing countries is heavily concentrated among primary and intermediate goods, the latter reflecting an increasing trend toward the geographic fragmentation of the production process and growing intraregional trade.[197] East Asia (excluding China) is the principal example of intraregional trade because of its status as a global manufacturing hub.[198] The global share of "South-South" trade is also significant and growing: in 2011, "South-South" trade accounted for 60 percent of East Asian trade and one-third of merchandise trade worldwide.[199]

Growth in developing-country merchandise trade has stimulated the expansion of these countries' maritime sectors. For example, in India, maritime cargo volume is forecast to grow at an annual rate of 8 percent through 2017. This has provided a rationale for increasing the terminal capacity of the country's state-owned sea ports; expanding coastal shipping services connecting ports along the country's perimeter; and setting up more frequent road and rail transport services between ports and inland destinations.[200] Similarly, in the Philippines, the country's main port terminal operator, International Container Terminal Services, Inc. has recently invested in a new inland container depot at the largest of Manila's three maritime ports. The new facility will help increase the cargo processing capacity at the port by nearly 20 percent to accommodate the country's growing volume of containerized exports and imports.[201] Overall, in 2011, 70 percent of the volume of containerized cargo was conveyed through the ports of 76 developing countries, and 15 of these ports were located in Asia. Although this share remained unchanged from the previous year, it was up from about 60 percent in 2005.[202]

---

[196] UNCTAD, *Key Trends in International Merchandise Trade, 2013,* 2013, 5. These numbers include trade between developed and developing countries, so there is some double-counting. In 2011, the total merchandise trade value was approximately $18 trillion.

[197] UNCTAD, *Key Trends in International Merchandise Trade, 2013,* 2013, 12–13.

[198] UNCTAD, *Key Trends in International Merchandise Trade, 2013,* 16 and 23. Here, East Asia includes the 10 countries within ASEAN as well as China, Japan, and South Korea. China's share of intraregional East Asian trade is relatively low, as it increasingly trades with developed countries outside of Asia.

[199] UNCTAD, *Key Trends in International Merchandise Trade, 2013,* 2013, 18, 21–25. The highest propensity for intraregional trade is among countries with complementary import and export profiles. Countries, such as those in East Asia, that are able to produce a range of technologically advanced, higher-value-added goods are more likely to trade with one another than with lower-income countries, such as those in sub-Saharan Africa, whose exports are less diverse. UNCTAD, *Key Trends in International Merchandise Trade, 2013,* 2013, 4.

[200] *Journal of Commerce,* "Heavy India Port Investment Needed," October 8, 2014.

[201] Knowler, "Manila Adds Yard Capacity," September 30, 2014.

[202] UNCTAD, *Review of Maritime Transport 2007,* 2007, 86, table 45, "Container Port Traffic"; UNCTAD, *Review of Maritime Transport 2013,* 2013, 89, table 4.1, "Container Port Throughput for 76 Developing."

Larger Container Ships (Megaships) are a Growing Feature of Maritime Trade

The global recession hit maritime firms hard financially.[203] Container shipping firms, in particular, experienced sharp decreases in demand, reducing their revenue by roughly 40 percent during the 2008–09 period.[204] As a result, such firms began to focus on ways to lower their per unit operating costs in order to maintain profitability: one strategy was to invest in larger container ships. These so-called megaships allow maritime firms to consolidate cargo and achieve greater economies of scale in the use of fuel, which can account for up to 60 percent of a ship's operating expenditures.[205] The largest container ship currently deployed is the Triple-E class.[206] It can carry 18,000 containers, 2,500 more than the next largest container ship (the "E Series") and three times the capacity of container ships built nearly two decades ago.[207] Maersk has purchased 20 Triple-E container ships, some of which are already in service on maritime routes between Asia and Europe, a market in which Maersk has a 22 percent share.[208] At the same time, CSCL (China Shipping Container Lines) has also procured five megaships, each with a capacity of 19,000 containers, which were scheduled for delivery at the end of 2014.[209] Some industry analysts suggest that the use of increasingly larger container ships will likely deepen the competitive divide in the container shipping industry. Firms

---

[203] WTO Secretariat, "Maritime Transport Services: Background Note," June 7, 2010, 6–7, and 20.

[204] Ibid., 7.

[205] Bonney, "Will Alliances Spark More Orders for Big Ships?" September 15, 2014; Tirschwell, "Next Up: Consolidation," August 27, 2014. Fuel cost expenditure ratios vary from between 20 and 60 percent depending on a ship's size, its fuel efficiency, and bunker (oil) prices, among other things. World Shipping Council, "Record Fuel Prices," May 2, 2008, 1.

[206] The name "Triple E" refers to these ships' economies of scale, energy efficiency, and environmental performance. Maersk, "Triple E: The Largest, Most Efficient Ship," n.d. (accessed February 18, 2015).

[207] Rodrigue, "Maritime Transportation," 2010, 11. The trend toward larger container ships is not new and has been stimulated, in part, by increased trade in containerized goods between China and Europe/North America. However, the use of larger container ships to engage in cost-based competition has become more intense over the years, as demand for containerized shipping services has increased and as maritime firms, with their high operating and capital costs, have become increasingly vulnerable to fluctuations in container freight rates. Bonney, "Will Alliances Spark More Orders for Big Ships?" September 15, 2014.

[208] A.P. Moller-Maersk A/S, *Annual Report 2013,* 2013, 27.

[209] It is interesting to note that ships of 18,000 TEUs or greater are too deep to pass through the Panama Canal, even after its planned expansion, and dock at U.S. ports, so they are currently not deployed between Asia and the United States. They can traverse the Suez Canal and are used to transport goods between Asia and Europe. Hakim, "Aboard a Cargo Colossus," October 3, 2014; Macguire, "Maersk 'Triple E,'" July 26, 2013.

deploying the largest ships will compete on the longest (and most lucrative) trade routes, while firms with smaller ships will be relegated to secondary, less profitable markets.[210]

Shipping Firms Form Global Alliances to Pool Resources and Increase Their Competitiveness

Another way shipping firms are working to remain cost competitive is through their participation in global alliances. Firms that participate in alliances sign vessel-sharing agreements that permit them to buy and sell cargo space on each other's ships, as well as to coordinate service schedules and the use of port terminal facilities. Alliances therefore allow shipping firms to combine resources, achieve economies of scale, and reduce capital costs.[211] Currently, the two largest container shipping alliances are the 2M Alliance, between A.P. Moller-Maersk (Denmark) and the Mediterranean Shipping Company (Switzerland), and the proposed Ocean Three (O3) Alliance,[212] formed by CMA-CGM (France), China Shipping Container Lines (CSCL), and the United Arab Shipping Company (UAE).[213] The members of these alliances will compete primarily on high-volume container trade lanes between Asia and Europe/North America.[214] At present, two other shipping alliances also serve these routes—the CKYHE and G6 alliances—which, combined with the trend towards larger container ships, underscores the increasing consolidation of service providers in these markets.[215] Overall, the four alliances, representing 16 major shipping lines, will account for 75 percent of the total container shipping capacity supplied worldwide.[216] While alliance formation may benefit large

---

[210] Mongelluzzo, "Consolidation—The Inevitable Result," September 10, 2014. Once more, the deployment of ever-larger container ships may result in the rerouting of these ships to ports that can accommodate larger vessels, in turn requiring the reconfiguration of certain maritime supply chains. UNCTAD, *Review of Maritime Transport 2013,* 2013, xiv.

[211] UNCTAD, *Review of Maritime Transport 2013,* 2013, xiii.

[212] The 2M Alliance has received regulatory approval from both EU antitrust authorities and the U.S. Federal Maritime Commission (FMC), whereas the Ocean Three alliance is still under regulatory review. Chee, "EU Regulators Clear Maersk, EU Shipping Alliances," June 3, 2014; FMC, "2M Agreement Clears FMC Regulatory Review," October 9, 2014. In its news release, the FMC states that its decision to approve the 2M Alliance was based on a determination that the agreement would not likely reduce competition or cause an "unreasonable increase in transportation cost or an unreasonable reduction in transportation service." The FMC's decision also places reporting requirements on members of the alliance.

[213] UASC, "UASC Signs Cooperation Agreements," September 9, 2014.

[214] Lavigne, "Sizing Up O3," September 15, 2014.

[215] The CKYHE alliance includes shipping firms COSCO (China); Kawasaki Kisen Kaisha, Ltd. ("K" Line) (Japan); Yang Ming Line (Taiwan); Hanjin Shipping (Korea); and Evergreen (Taiwan). The G6 Alliance includes APL (Singapore); Hyundai Merchant Marine (Korea); Orient Overseas Container Line (Hong Kong); Nippon Yusen Kaisha (NYK) Line (Japan); and Hapag-Lloyd (Germany). Mongelluzzo, "Consolidation—The Inevitable Result of Ever-Larger Ships," September 10, 2014.

[216] Wallis and Zawadzki, "2M Alliance Clears Regulatory Hurdles," October 9, 2014.

container shipping firms, they may also lead to a sharp decrease in the number of midsize providers that can effectively compete on certain maritime routes.[217]

Trade Trends

Cross-border Trade

In 2013, U.S. exports of maritime transport services (box 4.3) reached $17.2 billion, and U.S. imports totaled $36.3 billion, resulting in a U.S. trade deficit of $19.1 billion (figure 4.1).[218] The deficit reflects the fact that most U.S. imports and exports are conveyed on foreign vessels.[219] In 2013, U.S. exports of maritime transport services grew by 0.7 percent, compared to an average annual decrease of 1 percent between 2008 and 2012. By contrast, U.S. maritime transport services imports increased by a robust 9.2 percent in 2013, reflecting a dramatic shift from the average annual decrease of 0.9 percent during the 2008–12 period.[220] The increase in U.S. imports in 2013 was likely the result of a rise in freight payments made by U.S. entities to operators of foreign vessels.[221] Overall, U.S. imports of maritime transport services accounted for 40 percent of total U.S. transportation services imports in 2013 (compared to 20 percent for U.S. exports).[222]

Box 4.3: Understanding BEA data on cross-border trade and affiliate transactions in maritime transport services

The Bureau of Economic Analysis (BEA) of the U.S. Department of Commerce (USDOC) prepared much of the data on cross-border trade cited in this chapter. For the purposes of this chapter, maritime transport services encompass freight transport and port services. Trade in these services stems from merchandise trade. For instance, exports of maritime freight transport services occur when U.S. ocean carriers[a] transport U.S. merchandise exports to foreign destinations or when U.S. ocean carriers convey cargo between two foreign ports.[b] By contrast, imports of freight transport services occur when foreign ocean carriers transport merchandise imports to the United States.[c] U.S. exports of port services include the value of goods (excluding fuel) and services procured by foreign ocean carriers while in U.S. seaports, whereas U.S. imports of port services include the value of goods and services procured by U.S carriers while in seaports of foreign countries.[d]

---

[217] UNCTAD, *Review of Maritime Transport 2013,* 2013, 53; *Journal of Commerce,* "Drewry: Demise of Small Carriers Cuts Competition," April 29, 2013. In 2013, about 30 countries were each served by three container shipping lines or less.

[218] BEA, *Survey of Current Business*, October 2014, 5–6. By contrast, in 2009, the U.S. deficit in maritime transport services was $9.6 billion.

[219] WTO, "Modest Trade Growth Anticipated for 2014 and 2015," April 14, 2014.

[220] USDOC, BEA, *Survey of Current Business,* October 2014, 5–6.

[221] BEA representative, email message to USITC staff, November 19, 2014.

[222] USDOC, BEA, *Survey of Current Business,* October 2014, 7.

The BEA also collects data on affiliate transactions in maritime transport services (referred to as "water transportation services"). The data are collected by BEA through surveys of U.S. direct investment abroad and foreign investment in the United States.[e] The BEA classifies these data according to the primary industry of the affiliate (as measured by sales) rather than the type of service.[f] For instance, if an affiliate whose main business was water transportation services also sold other services, the BEA would record all of the affiliate's sales under water transportation services. In general, affiliate transactions in water transportation services are categorized under North America Industry Classification System (NAICS) 4839, which includes the water transportation of passengers and cargo (except petroleum and related products) using ships, barges, and boats in deep-sea, coastal, or inland waterways.[g]

[a] According to BEA, a U.S. ocean carrier is one that is operated by crew members whose country of residence is the United States, but it may not necessarily be U.S. owned or fly the U.S. flag.

[b] Under the balance-of-payments convention, the importer is said to assume ownership of the goods when they cross the border of the exporting country, and is thus responsible for all transportation costs from then on. Therefore, sales by U.S. carriers for the transport of U.S. imports are excluded from U.S. transportation exports because, by this convention, they represent transactions between U.S. parties. Similarly, payments to foreign carriers for transporting U.S. exports are not included in U.S. imports because they represent foreign residents paying foreign airlines, ocean carriers, or trucking firms. USDOC, BEA, *Survey of Current Business,* October 1998, 78.

[c] Transactions involving a U.S. resident contracting with a foreign carrier to transport goods between two foreign ports are not included in calculations of U.S. imports of maritime transport services. BEA representative, email message to USITC staff, November 24, 2014.

[d] BEA representative, email message to USITC staff, November 24, 2014.

[e] Specifically, the BEA collects data on transactions by U.S. affiliates of foreign companies using forms BE-12 (Benchmark Survey) and BE-15 (Annual Survey). For transactions of foreign affiliates of U.S. firms, the BEA collects data using forms BE-10 (Benchmark Survey) and BE-15 (Annual Survey).

[f] BEA representative, email message to USITC staff, November 21, 2014.

[g] Ibid., November 24, 2014.

Figure 4.1: Maritime transport services: U.S. cross-border trade in maritime transport services resulted in a U.S. trade deficit each year during 2009–13

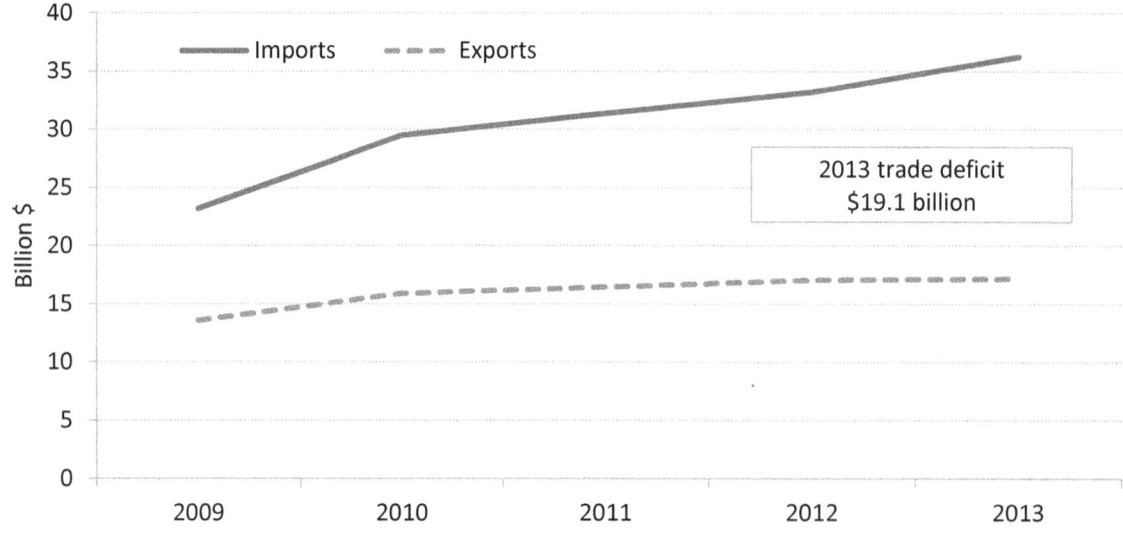

Source: USDOC, BEA, *Survey of Current Business,* October 2014, 1–2, table 1. (See appendix table B.12).

The top five countries for U.S. exports of maritime transport services in 2013 were unchanged from the previous year. They were Japan, accounting for 13 percent of total U.S. exports, followed by Taiwan (9 percent), Germany (8 percent), South Korea (7 percent) and China (6 percent) (figure 4.2). The United States posted trade deficits with each of these countries (figure 4.3). The largest deficit was with Japan ($2.9 billion), followed by Germany and South Korea ($1.3 billion each). Correspondingly, the top five U.S. liner cargo trading partners were similar to the leading five markets for U.S. exports of maritime transport services. In descending order by volume of cargo carried, they were China, Japan, South Korea, Taiwan, and Hong Kong (China),[223] with Germany ranking sixth.[224] These markets may have an advantage in the provision of maritime transport services, as they are also among the largest shipbuilding economies in the world.[225]

---

[223] FMC, *52nd Annual Report,* Fiscal Year 2013, 24. Data for Hong Kong are captured separately because Hong Kong is a major maritime transshipment center. Volume is measured in TEUs.

[224] FMC, *52nd Annual Report,* Fiscal Year 2013, 24. Data are from 2012.

[225] Rowe, "Shipbuilding Market Overview," March 19, 2013. Data are from 2012. In that year, China, Japan, and South Korea ranked as the first-, second- and third-largest global shipbuilders; Germany ranked fourth and Taiwan, sixth.

Figure 4.2: Maritime transport services: Japan was the leading market for U.S. cross-border exports and imports of maritime transport services in 2013

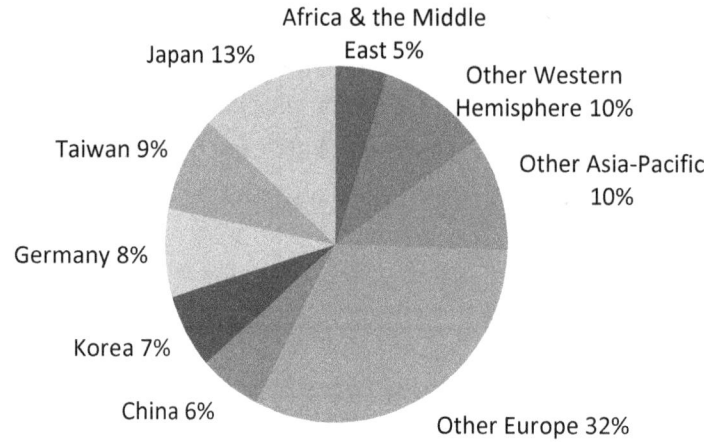

U.S. exports
Total = $17.2 billion

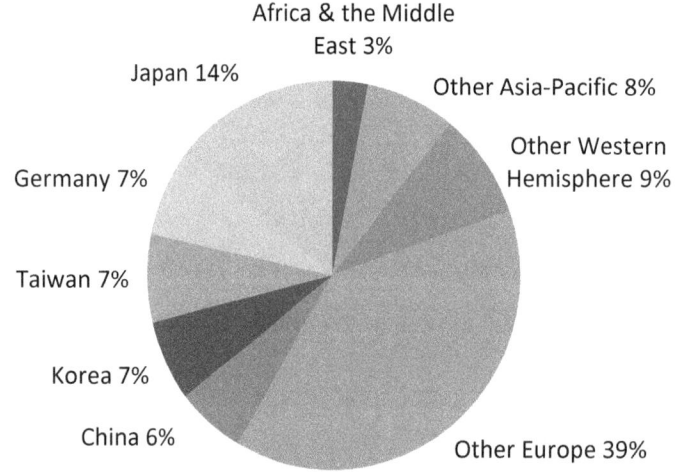

U.S. imports
Total = $36.3 billion

Source: USDOC, BEA, *Survey of Current Business*, October 2014, 6, table 3.2. (See appendix table B.13).
Note: Figures may not total to 100 percent due to rounding.

Figure 4.3: Maritime transport services: In 2013, the United States posted its largest trade deficit in maritime transport services with Japan

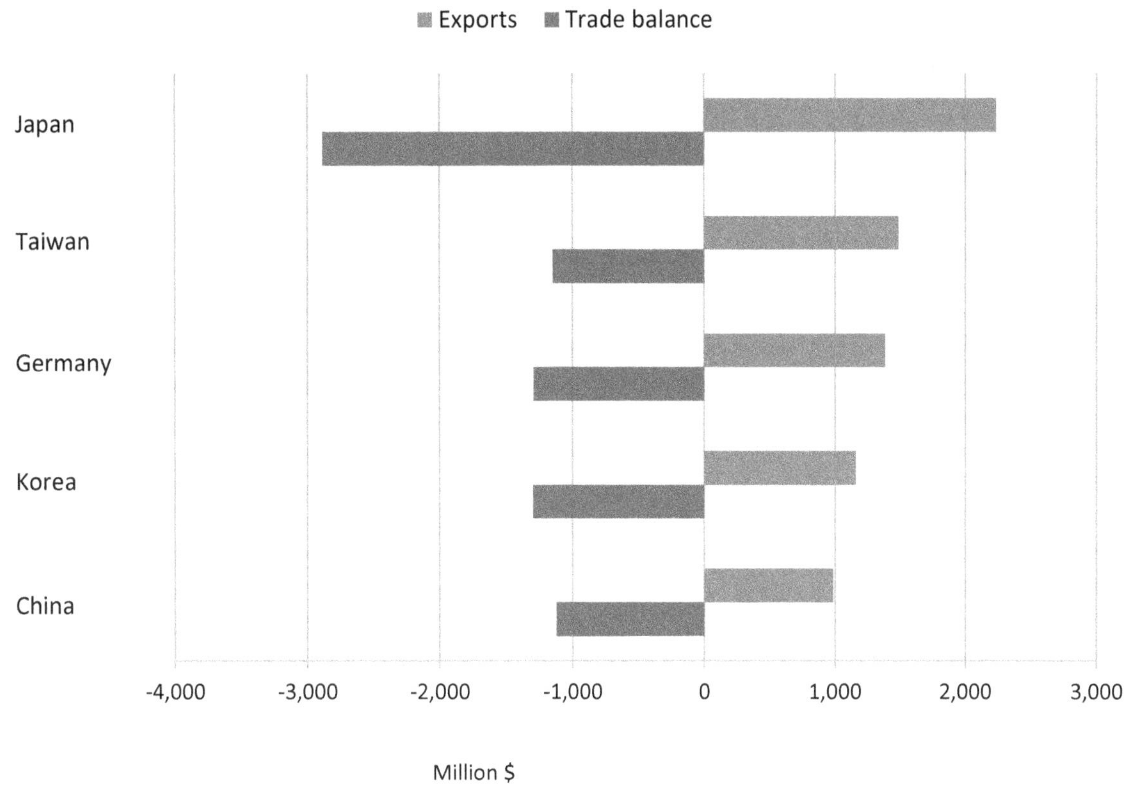

Exports ■ Trade balance

Source: USDOC, BEA, *Survey of Current Business,* October 2014, table 2.2, 6. (See appendix table B.14).

Affiliate Transactions

In 2012, total sales for foreign affiliates of U.S. maritime transport services firms were $8.7 billion. This represented a decrease of 4.4 percent from the previous year, consistent with an average annual decrease of 4 percent during the 2008–11 period (figure 4.4). By comparison, total sales of U.S. affiliates of foreign maritime transport services firms in 2012 reached $6.5 billion. While this was an increase of 1.1 from the previous year, it, too, was significantly lower than the average annual growth rate of nearly 28 percent recorded during 2008–11.[226] The large growth in U.S. affiliate sales for 2008–11 partly reflects an increase in

Figure 4.4: Maritime transport services: Services supplied by affiliates of U.S.-owned maritime transport services firms abroad exceeded services supplied by foreign-owned affiliates in the United States in 2012

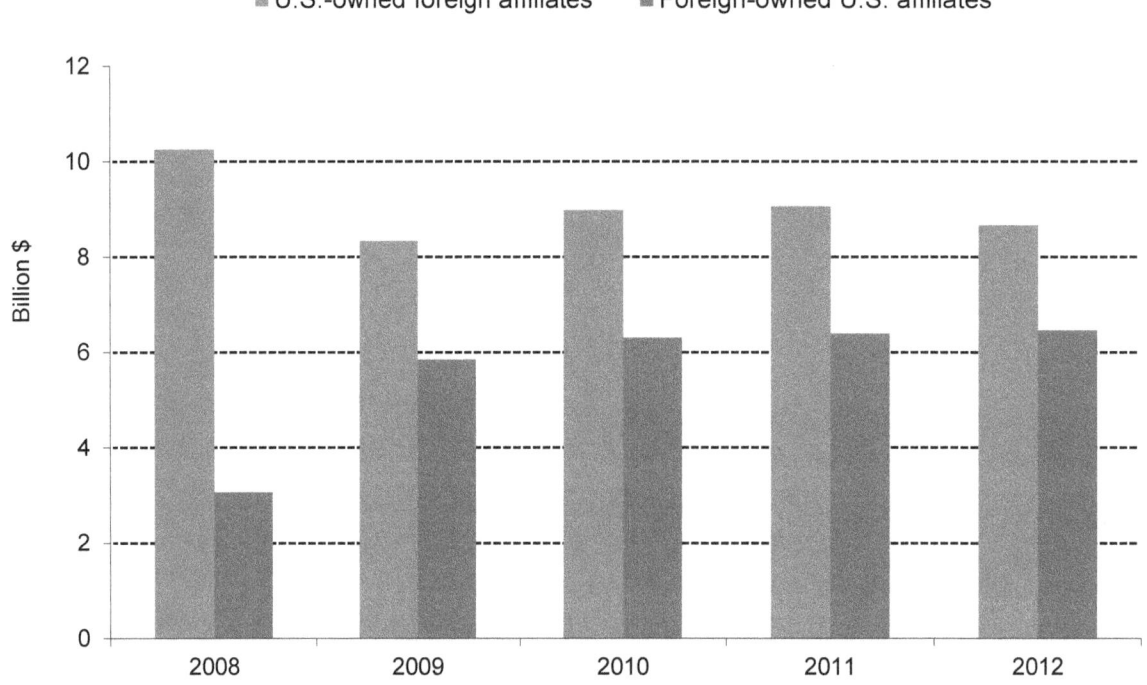

Source: USDOC, BEA, International Data, Interactive tables: "Table 3.1. Services Supplied to Foreign Persons by U.S. MNEs Through Their MOFAs, by Industry of Affiliate and by Country of Affiliate," (accessed November 25, 2014). (See appendix table B.15).

---

[226] USDOC, BEA, International Data, Interactive tables: "Table 3.1. Services Supplied to Foreign Persons," (accessed November 25, 2014).

both freight rates and volume of maritime shipping between 2009 and 2010.[227] Much of the country-level data on affiliate transactions in maritime transport services has been suppressed by BEA to avoid disclosure of individual company information. However, available data indicate that the United Kingdom is the largest market for foreign affiliate sales by U.S. maritime transport services firms in Europe, accounting for roughly 78 percent of such sales in both 2011 and 2012.[228]

Outlook

The maritime transport services industry will continue to be affected by changes in global supply chains, an increase in shipping capacity with the deployment of ever-larger container ships, and the consolidation of service suppliers through global alliances. For example, as developing countries, such as those in Africa and Asia, slowly replace China as manufacturing centers for labor-intensive goods, these countries will play an important role in reshaping maritime transport routes.[229] In addition, the increasing participation of developing countries in global trade will continue to stimulate greater investment in port infrastructure. Such investment will be aimed at expanding port capacity on the one hand and improving port productivity (i.e., the ability of a port to handle a growing volume of cargo cost-efficiently) on the other.[230] Already, port construction projects are underway in places like Côte d'Ivoire (Abidjan), Cambodia (Phnom Penh), Ghana (Tema), India (Dugarajapatnam), and Tanzania (Bagamoyo), to prepare these countries to take on a more expansive role in maritime trade.[231]

Separately, the trend towards large container ships appears likely to continue in the near future, but this could also exacerbate the already strong potential for container carrying capacity to outstrip demand.[232] The latter may stimulate shipping firms to consolidate further through alliance formation—provided that such alliances continue to survive despite close

---

[227] BEA representative, email message to USITC staff, November 21, 2014. In addition, according to a BEA representative, there were two other reasons for the large increase in U.S. affiliate sales of maritime transport services firms during the 2008–11 period: (1) affiliates that were previously classified in the industry in which they recorded the largest sales were reclassified under water transportation services; and (2) affiliates of foreign-based water transportation services firms garnered a larger share of their total sales in the United States during the 2008–11 period than in other foreign markets. USDOC, BEA, International Data, Interactive tables: "Table 3.1. Services Supplied to Foreign Persons" (accessed November 25, 2014).

[228] USDOC, BEA, *Survey of Current Business,* October 2014, 20–23.

[229] UNCTAD, *Review of Maritime Transport 2013,* 2013, xii.

[230] Barnard, "Ports Expected to Be at Center," November 19, 2014.

[231] UNCTAD, *Review of Maritime Transport 2013,* 2013, 95 and 97; Egan, "Ghana Port to Triple Capacity," November 18, 2012.

[232] Waters, "Competition Implications of 2M and Mega-Alliances," November 18, 2014; Brooks, "Record 2015 Ship Deliveries," October 15, 2014.

scrutiny by regulators.[233] Moreover, the widespread deployment of increasingly large container ships will likely be hampered by port infrastructure, at least in the short term. In the longer term, infrastructure upgrades at certain ports may alleviate some of this concern. So, too, will the completion of the Panama Canal expansion in 2016, which will permit the passage of container ships of up to 13,000 TEUs.[234]

Finally, market conditions in the maritime transport services industry may also be affected by a growing emphasis on environmental protection and ongoing efforts to enhance maritime cargo security. For instance, in July 2011, the International Maritime Organization adopted new measures to augment energy efficiency and reduce the release of greenhouse gas emissions from ships.[235] These measures entered into force on January 1, 2013; they require that ships deployed beginning in 2015 demonstrate a 10 percent improvement in fuel efficiency by 2020, and a 30 percent improvement by 2030.[236] The new environmental standards may confer a competitive advantage on countries with large shipping firms, such as Maersk, that already use the newest, most fuel-efficient ships.[237] Discussion continues as to how countries (and ship owners) would be penalized if they are unable to meet the new emissions standards.[238] At the same time, efforts to improve maritime cargo security—such as under the EU's Authorized Economic Operator program—continue to place more data-reporting requirements on shipping firms.[239] While many of these requirements are necessary to assess potential supply chain risks, they also impose additional costs on maritime transport services providers.[240]

---

[233] Leach, "FMC's Lidinsky Calls for Global Regulation," November 7, 2014.

[234] UNCTAD, *Review of Maritime Transport 2013,* 2013, 96. There are also plans to build a competing canal in Nicaragua, which would be designed to accommodate the now largest container ship in service, the Triple-E vessel. The canal will be built and operated by the Hong Kong Nicaragua Canal Development Investment Co., Ltd., which has been granted a 50-year concession (with the option to renew for another 50 years) by the government of Nicaragua. The canal may take up to 10 years to complete, and there are certain environmental and other concerns regarding its development. Leach, "Are Nicaragua Canal Plans Driven by Geopolitics?" October 20, 2014.

[235] UNCTAD, *Review of Maritime Transport 2012,* 2012, 97. The measures were added as an amendment to the International Convention for the Prevention of Pollution from Ships (MARPOL 73/78).

[236] NPR, "U.N. Panel Sets Emission Standards," July 15, 2011.

[237] Waters, "Competition Implications of 2M and Mega-Alliances," November 18, 2014.

[238] NPR, "U.N. Panel Sets Emission Standards," July 15, 2011.

[239] On January 31, 2013, an agreement between the United States and the EU entered into force providing reciprocal benefits to "safe traders" that are registered under either the United States' Customs-Trade Partnership Against Terrorism (C-TPAT) program or the EU's Authorized Economic Operator program. UNCTAD, *Review of Maritime Transport 2012,* 2012, 97.

[240] Deloitte, "The Authorised Economic Operator (AEO) Concept," August 13, 2013, 7.

Bibliography

3PL News. "After a Year Shaped by Global Crisis, CMA CGM Returns to Profit," May 4, 2010. http://www.3plnews.com/ocean-freight/after-a-year-shaped-by-global-crisis-cma-cgm-returns-to-profit.html.

African Development Bank. "Reforms and the Regulatory Framework of African Ports." Chapter 3 in *Africa Development Report, 2010*. Oxford, UK: Oxford University Press, 2010. http://www.afdb.org/fileadmin/uploads/afdb/Documents/Publications/African%20Development%20Report%202010.pdf.

A.P. Moller-Maersk A/S. *Annual Report 2013*, 2013. http://files.shareholder.com/downloads/ABEA-3GG91Y/0x0x731491/fb0012ef-15f0-4fda-80e0-d9a1b00b698e/Annual_Report_2013.pdf.

Association of Southeast Asian Nations (ASEAN). "2007 Agreement on Maritime Transport between the Governments of the Member Countries of the Association of Southeast Asian Nations and the Government of the People's Republic of China," November 2, 2007. http://www.asean.org/communities/asean-economic-community/item/agreement-on-maritime-transport-between-the-governments-of-the-member-countries-of-the-association-of-southeast-asian-nations-and-the-government-of-the-people-s-republic-of-china.

Barnard, Bruce. "Ports Expected to Be at Center of Container Shipping Strategy." *Journal of Commerce*, November 19, 2014. http://www.joc.com/print/2765996.

Bonney, Joseph. "Will Alliances Spark More Orders for Big Ships?" *Journal of Commerce*, September 15, 2014. http://www.joc.com/print2760751?mgs1=72bhfixb2.

Brooks, Chris. "Record 2015 Ship Deliveries Likely to Create Another Tough Year for Carriers." *Journal of Commerce*, October 15, 2014. http://www.joc.com/maritime-news/ships-shipbuilding/record-2015-ship-deliveries-likely-create-another-tough-year-carriers_20141015.html.

Bureau Van Dijk. ORBIS Database. "United Arab Shipping Company (S.A.G.)." https://orbis.bvdinfo.com/version-20141120/Report.serv?_CID=441&context=7ZQ52X36T9HMA3Y&SeqNr=0 (accessed November 25, 2014) (paid subscription required).

Chee, Foo Yun. "EU Regulators Clear Maersk, EU Shipping Alliances." *gCaptain.com*, June 3, 2014. http://gcaptain.com/eu-regulators-clear-maersk-nippon-yusen-shipping-alliances/.

China COSCO Holdings Company Limited. *Annual Report 2013*, 2013. http://en.chinacosco.com/col/col1096/index.html.

CSAV. "European Commission Approves Merger." http://www.csav.com/en/News/Pages/CSAV-welcomes-EU-approval-for-merger-with-Hapag-Lloyd.aspx (accessed September 19, 2014).

Deloitte. "The Authorised Economic Operator (AEO) Concept: Blessing or Curse?" *Deloitte Customs and Global Trade Newsletter* 1, no. 4 (August 13, 2013). https://www.google.com/#q=AEO+costs+deloitte.

DP World. *Annual Report and Accounts, 2013*, 2013. http://web.dpworld.com/investor-centre/annual-report/.

———. "Our Business," n.d. http://web.dpworld.com/our-business/ (accessed September 29, 2014).

Drewry. "Drewry's Top Ten Global Terminal Operators," August 27, 2013. http://www.drewry.co.uk/news.php?id=232.

Dupin, Chris. "China Seeks Boost to Shipping Industry." *American Shipper*, September 4, 2014.

Economic Times. "Hutchinson Sells 20% Port Stake to Rival," April 22, 2006. http://articles.economictimes.indiatimes.com/2006-04-22/news/27429134_1_port-assets-hutchison-whampoa-hutchison-port-holdings.

Egan, Corianne. "Ghana Port to Triple Capacity with $1.5 Billion Expansion." *Journal of Commerce*, November 18, 2012. http://www.joc.com/print/2765886?destination=node/2765886.

Everett, Sophia, and Ross Robinson. "Port Reform: The Australian Experience." Chapter 12 in *Devolution, Port Governance and Port Performance,* edited by Mary R. Brooks and Kevin Cullinane. Research in Transportation Economics vol. 17. Amsterdam: Elsevier, 2007. http://202.114.89.60/resource/pdf/2117.pdf.

Evergreen Marine Corp. (Taiwan) Ltd. *2013 Annual Report*, 2013. http://www.evergreen-marine.com/tbf1/jsp/TBF1_FinancialReports.jsp.

Federal Maritime Commission (FMC). "2M Agreement Clears FMC Regulatory Review." News release, October 9, 2014. http://www.fmc.gov/NR14-12/.

———. *50th Annual Report*, Fiscal Year 2011.

Federal Maritime Commission (FMC). 5*2nd Annual Report*, Fiscal Year 2013.

FIS.com. "P&O Nedlloyd Company Headquarters," n.d. http://www.fis.com/fis/companies/details.asp?l=e&filterby=companies&=&country_id=&page=1&company_id=18444 (accessed September 16, 2014).

Hakim, Danny. "Aboard a Cargo Colossus." *New York Times*, October 3, 2014. http://www.nytimes.com/2014/10/05/business/international/aboard-a-cargo-colossus-maersks-new-container-ships.html.

Hanjin Shipping. "Bulk Vessel Fleet," n.d. https://www.hanjin.com/hanjin/CUP_HOM_1250.do?sessLocale=en (accessed October 3, 2014).

———. "Hanjin Shipping Holdings Company Limited" (accessed September 26, 2014). http://www.corporateinformation.com/Company-Snapshot.aspx?cusip=C41008820.

Hanjin Shipping Holdings. *2011 Business Report,* December 31, 2011. www.hanjin-holdings.com/.../businessreport/BNR20120529094921.PDF.

Hapag-Lloyd. "CP Ships Finalizes Plans for New Australasian Services." Press release, December 27, 2005. http://www.hapag-lloyd.de/en/press_and_media/press_release_page_9500.html.

———. *Annual Report 2013*, 2013. https://www.hapag-lloyd.com/en/.../news_page_34211.htm.

Haarmeyer, David, and Peter Yorke. "Port Privatization: An International Perspective." Reason Foundation, Policy Study No. 156, April 1993. http://reason.org/files/6a983123788632131171e022e6466a7a.pdf.

HKTDC. "US, China Sign Historic Maritime Agreement." *Business Alert-US,* no. 25, December 24, 2003. http://info.hktdc.com/alert/us0325.htm.

Hoover's. "China COSCO Holdings Company Limited Revenue and Financial Data," n.d. http://www.hoovers.com/company-information/cs/revenue-financial.China_COSCO_Holdings_Company_Limited.1251662e4599a7cd.html (accessed October 1, 2014).

———. "Evergreen Marine Corporation (Taiwan) Ltd. Revenue and Financial Data," n.d. http://www.hoovers.com/company-information/cs/revenue-financial.Evergreen_Marine_Corporation.54fc34668bcd3166.html (accessed October 1, 2014).

Hutchinson Port Holdings. "Company Profile," n.d. http://www.hph.com/webpg.aspx?id=87 (accessed September 26, 2014).

Journal of Commerce. "Drewry: Demise of Small Carriers Cuts Competition," April 29, 2013. http://www.joc.com/maritime-news/container-lines/drewry-demise-small-carriers-cuts-competition_20130429.html.

———. "Heavy India Port Investment Needed to Handle Expected Growth Volumes," October 8, 2014. http://www.joc.com/port-news/international-ports/heavy-india-port-investment-needed-handle-expected-growth-volumes_20141008.html

Kane, Frank. "DP World Demands S&P Withdraw Credit Rating." *National Business*, May 18, 2012. http://www.thenational.ae/business/industry-insights/finance/dp-world-demands-s-p-withdraw-credit-rating.

Kent, Paul E. "Port Reform, Privatization, and Regulation." PowerPoint presentation for the U.S. Agency for International Development (USAID), December 17, 2008. https://www.google.com/#q=kent+port+reform+privatization+and+regulation.

Knowler, Greg. "Manila Adds Yard Capacity to Cope with Growth in Trade." *Journal of Commerce*, September 30, 2014. http://www.joc.com/port-news/asian-ports/manila-adds-yard-capacity-cope-growth-trade_20140930.html.

Lavigne, Grace M. "Sizing up O3." *Journal of Commerce*, September 15, 2014. http://www.joc.com/print/2760766?mgs1=242ahfixb6.

Leach, Peter T. "EU Approves Merger of Hapag-Lloyd, CSAV, with Caveats." *Journal of Commerce*, September 11, 2014. http://www.joc.com/maritime-news/container-lines/hapag-lloyd/eu-approves-merger-hapag-lloyd-csav_20140911.html.

———. "Are Nicaragua Canal Plans Driven by Geopolitics?" *Journal of Commerce*, October 20, 2014. http://www.joc.com/maritime-news/trade-lanes/are-nicaragua-canal-plans-driven-geopolitics_20141020.html.

———. "FMC's Lidinsky Calls for Global Regulation of Ship Alliances." *Journal of Commerce*, November 7, 2014. http://www.joc.com/regulation-policy/transportation-regulations/international-transportation-regulations/fmc%E2%80%99s-lidinsky-calls-global-regulation-ship-alliances_20141107.html?destination=node/2765086.

Leonel, Andrea. "South-South Trade—Rewiring the Global Economy." J.P. Morgan, n.d. https://www.jpmorgan.com/tss/General/South-South_Trade_Rewiring_the_Global_Economy/1320504817166 (accessed September 10, 2014).

Maersk. "Triple E: The Largest, Most Efficient Ship in the World," n.d. http://www.maerskline.com/en-us/shipping-services/dry-cargo/our-network/triple-e-card-cascading (accessed February 18, 2015).

Macguire, Eoghan. "Maersk 'Triple E': Introducing the World's Biggest Ship." CNN.com, July 26, 2013. http://edition.cnn.com/2013/06/26/business/maersk-triple-e-biggest-ship/index.html.

McGuire, Greg, Michael Schuele, and Tina Smith. "Restrictiveness of International Trade in Maritime Services." In *Impediments to Trade in Services*, edited by Christopher Findlay and Warren Tony. London: Routledge, 2000.

Mongelluzzo, Bill. "Consolidation—The Inevitable Result of Ever-Larger Ships, Analyst Predicts." *Journal of Commerce*, September 10, 2014. http://www.joc.com/print/2760371?mgs1=206bhdyjMt.

Moody's Investor Services. *Privately Managed Port Companies,* May 13, 2013. http://web.dpworld.com/wp-content/uploads/2014/05/Privately-Managed-Port-Companies-1305.pdf.

———. "Rating Action: Moody's Affirms PSA International and PSA Corporation's Ratings," Press release, October 17, 2013. https://www.moodys.com/research/Moodys-affirms-PSA-International-and-PSA-Corporations-ratings--PR_284698.

Motorship. "CMA CGM Acquires Delmas," September 13, 2005. http://www.motorship.com/news101/industry-news/cma-cgm-acquires-delmas.

Neptune Orient Lines Limited. *Annual Report 2013*, 2013. http://www.nol.com.sg/wps/portal/nol/investorrelations/reportsandannouncements/annualreports.

NPR. "U.N. Panel Sets Emission Standards for Cargo Ships," July 15, 2011. http://www.npr.org/2011/07/15/138166739/u-n-panel-sets-emissions-standards-for-cargo-ships.

Online Asia Times. "A New Era in Asian Shipping," September 2, 2000. http://www.atimes.com/se-asia/BI02Ae03.html.

Organisation for Economic Co-operation and Development (OECD). *Regulatory Issues in International Maritime Transport*, 2001.

———. Quarterly National Accounts database. http://stats.oecd.org/Index.aspx?QueryName=350&QueryType=View&Lang=en (accessed February 12, 2015).

PSA company website. "Our Business," n.d. https://www.singaporepsa.com/our-business/terminals (accessed February 13, 2015).

Rodrigue, Jean-Paul. "The Geography of Transport Systems: Public and Private Roles in Port Management." Hofstra University, n.d. https://people.hofstra.edu/geotrans/eng/ch4en/conc4en/tbl_public_privte_roles_ports.html (accessed November 5, 2014).

———. "Maritime Transportation: Drivers for the Shipping and Port Industries." International Transport Forum paper, 2010. http://www.internationaltransportforum.org/pub/pdf/10FP02.pdf.

Rodrigue, Jean-Paul, and Theo Notteboom. "Global Networks in the Container Terminal Operating Industry, Part I: How Global Are Global Terminal Operators?" *Port Technology International* 49, Spring 2011. http://www.porttechnology.org/images/uploads/technical_papers/10-14.pdf.

Rowe, Martin. "Shipbuilding Market Overview." Clarkson Asia. PowerPoint presentation to Marine Money, Hong Kong, March 19, 2013. www.marinemoney.com/sites/all/.../0955B%20Martin%20Rowe.pdf.

Steelguru.com. "Hagag Lloyd Operating Profit Up by 19 Percent YoY," March 27, 2009. http://www.steelguru.com/international_news/Hapag_Lloyd_2008_operating_profit_up_by_19_percent_YoY/87753.html.

Tirschwell, Peter. "Next Up: Consolidation." *Journal of Commerce*, August 27, 2014. http://www.joc.com/maritime-news/container-lines/next-consolidation_20140827.html.

Turpin, François-Marc. "PPP in Ports, Landlord Port Model." PowerPoint presentation for Logmos Project, Tbilisi, Georgia, April 12, 2013. http://www.traceca-org.org/uploads/media/04_Module_C_PPP_Francois_Marc_Turpin_new.pdf.

United Arab Shipping Company (UASC). "UASC Signs Cooperation Agreements with CSCL and CMA CGM." News release, September 9, 2014. http://www.uasc.net/en/news/140909/uasc-signs-cooperation-agreements-cscl-and-cma-cgm.

United Nations (UN). "Provisional Central Product Classification, Series M No. 7," 1991.

United Nations Conference on Trade and Development (UNCTAD). *Review of Maritime Transport 2012*, 2012. http://unctad.org/en/pages/PublicationWebflyer.aspx?publicationid=380.

———. *Key Trends in International Merchandise Trade*, 2013. http://unctad.org/en/pages/PublicationWebflyer.aspx?publicationid=686.

———. *Review of Maritime Transport 2013*, 2013. Figure 1.3(b), "Participation of Developing Economies in World Seaborne Trade, Selected Years (percentage share in world tonnage)." http://unctad.org/en/pages/PublicationWebflyer.aspx?publicationid=753.

———. *Review of Maritime Transport 2007*, 2007. Table 45, "Container Port Traffic for 62 Developing Countries and Territories, 2004, 2005 and 2006." http://unctad.org/en/pages/PublicationArchive.aspx?publicationid=1676.

———. *Review of Maritime Transport 2014*, 2014. Figure 2.3, "Ownership of the World Fleet, as of 1 January 2014 (dwt)." http://unctad.org/en/pages/PublicationWebflyer.aspx?publicationid=1068.

———. *Review of Maritime Transport 2014,* 2014. Figure 2.5, "Top 20 Shipowning Nations, Beneficial Ownership, 1 January 2014 (1,000 dwt by country/economy of ownership)." http://unctad.org/en/pages/PublicationWebflyer.aspx?publicationid=1068.

———. *Review of Maritime Transport 2014,* 2014. Table 2.4, "The 50 Leading Liner Companies, 1 January 2014 (number of ships and total shipboard capacity deployed, in TEUs, ranked by TEU)." http://unctad.org/en/pages/PublicationWebflyer.aspx?publicationid=1068.

———. *Review of Maritime Transport 2014,* 2014. Table 2.5, "The 35 Flags of Registration with the Largest Registered Fleets, as of 1 January 2014 (Dwt). http://unctad.org/en/pages/PublicationWebflyer.aspx?publicationid=1068.

———. *Review of Maritime Transport 2014,* 2014.Table 4.1, "Container Port Throughput for 76 Developing Countries/Territories and Economies in Transition for Years 2010, 2011 and 2012 (twenty-foot equivalent units)."

U.S. Department of Commerce (USDOC). Bureau of Economic Analysis (BEA). *Survey of Current Business*, October 1998. http://www.bea.gov/scb/pdf/INTERNAT/INTSERV/1998/1098srv.pdf.

———. *Survey of Current Business*, October 2014. http://www.bea.gov/scb/pdf/2014/10%20October/1014_international_services.pdf.

———. International Data, Interactive tables. Table 3.1: "Services Supplied to Foreign Persons by U.S. MNEs through Their MOFAs, by Industry of Affiliate and by Country of Affiliate." http://www.bea.gov/iTable/iTable.cfm?ReqID=62&step=1#reqid=62&step=9&isuri=1&6210=4.

U.S. Department of Transportation (USDOT). Maritime Administration (MARAD). "Agreement on Maritime Transport between the Government of the United States of America and the Government of the Federative Republic of Brazil," September 30, 2005. http://www.marad.dot.gov/documents/IA_US_Brazil_Maritime_Agreement_2005-English.pdf.

U.S. International Trade Commission. *Recent Trends in U.S. Services Trade: 2000 Annual Report,* USITC Publication 3306. Washington, D.C.: USITC, 2000.

Wallis, Keith, and Zawadzki, Sabina. "2M Alliance Clears Regulatory Hurdles, Plans January 2015 Start." *gCaptain.com*, October 9, 2014. http://gcaptain.com/2m-alliance-to-start-in-january-2015/.

Waters, Will. "Competition Implications of 2M and Mega-Alliances." *Lloyd's Loading List*, November 18, 2014. http://www.lloydsloadinglist.com/freight-directory/news/competition-implications-of-2m-and-mega-alliances/20018120434.htm?source=ezine&utm_source=Lloyd%27s+Loading+List+Daily+News+Bulletin&utm_campaign=a1d227b0ee-Wed_30_July7_30_2014&utm_medium=email&utm_term=0_1a5c244239-a1d227b0ee-256627597#.VG4kpclFo3m.

World Shipping Council. "Record Fuel Prices Place Stress on Ocean Shipping," May 2, 2008. http://www.worldshipping.org/pdf/wsc_fuel_statement_final.pdf.

———. Glossary of Industry Terms, n.d. http://www.worldshipping.org/about-the-industry/glossary-of-industry-terms (accessed October 3, 2014).

———. "Trade Routes (TEU Shipped), 2012." http://www.worldshipping.org/about-the-industry/global-trade/trade-routes (accessed October 3, 2014).

World Trade Organization (WTO). I-TIP Services Database, n.d. http://i-tip.wto.org/services/(S(v0n14o1w22kmo5dqkdf0gpww))/SearchResultGats.aspx (accessed October 8, 2014).

———. "Modest Trade Growth Anticipated for 2014 and 2015 Following Two Year Slump." Press release, April 14, 2014. http://www.wto.org/english/news_e/pres14_e/pr721_e.htm.

———. Secretariat. "Maritime Transport Services: Background Note by the Secretariat." S/C/W/315, June 7, 2010. http://www.wto.org/english/tratop_e/serv_e/transport_e/transport_maritime_e.htm.

Chapter 5
Retail Services

Summary

As a fundamental commercial activity, retailing accounts for a significant proportion of global output and employment. Global retail sales have posted strong annual growth since the global recession of 2008–09. In the United States, more than a tenth of the population is directly employed in retail services, which account for nearly 7 percent of GDP.[241] The United States was the leading retail market in 2014 and home to the largest global retailing firms. However, retail sales grew faster in developing countries such as China, which is projected to become the world's largest retail market in the coming years.[242]

Digital technology and the Internet are dramatically transforming the retail sector. E-commerce is the fastest-growing segment in global retail, and the rapid adoption of mobile technology around the globe is providing consumers with a multitude of information and shopping choices. In response, retailers are evolving into multichannel suppliers, offering a range of integrated online and in-store services to meet the expectations of their digitally empowered consumers.

The value of retail services supplied by U.S.-owned foreign affiliates increased in 2012, continuing the strong growth of the years following the global recession. Leading markets corresponded to leading U.S. trading partners, including Canada, the United Kingdom, and Mexico. Services supplied by foreign-owned retailers in the United States similarly experienced robust growth as the U.S. economy recovered from the recession. U.S. investment in foreign retail operations also grew substantially in recent years, in part in order to enter faster-growing international markets, including developing countries. In the coming years, expanding output, rising incomes, and burgeoning middle classes in many of the faster-growing developing countries, including China, will likely shift the center of global retailing away from developed markets to emerging economies, particularly in the Asia-Pacific region.

Introduction

Retailers are the critical link between producers and consumers, and are the final stage in the merchandise distribution process. When shoppers make a retail purchase, they are paying for

---

[241] Note that GDP refers to real GDP of private industries.
[242] EIU, "Retail in China," 2014, 2.

both the merchandise and the distribution services associated with it. Retail services can include transportation, warehousing, real estate costs, advertising, and other associated activities. Retailers operate via physical stores or, increasingly, through multiple other channels, such as the Internet (e-commerce), catalogs, television, and direct selling.[243] Retailing accounts for a substantial share of output and employment in most countries. In the United States, the retail industry employed 15.4 million people in 2013 (representing 11.1 percent of nonfarm employment)[244] and accounted for 6.6 percent of value added as a share of GDP ($902.8 billion).[245] According to the National Retail Federation (NRF), a total of 3.8 million U.S. retail establishments employed 29 million workers that year.[246]

Demand for retail services reflects broader factors in the economy, such as consumer income, the performance of the economy, and consumers' expectations about future income, as well as a myriad of consumer preferences. Retail supply factors include the quality of infrastructure and transport networks for moving merchandise to stores or warehouses; access to real estate suitable for store sites; and the availability of workers to staff stores, back-end operations, and Internet operations. For the ever-expanding e-commerce subsector, additional supply factors include consumers' access to the Internet and mobile phone services; the availability of logistics, shipping, and other fulfillment services; and the tax treatment of online transactions, among others.

Market Conditions in Global Retail Services

Global retail sales revenue was $19.7 trillion in 2014, an increase of 22.4 percent from 2010.[247] The United States was the world's largest retail market in 2014, with revenue totaling $3.7 trillion, or 18.7 percent of the global total (figure 5.1).[248] While the U.S. market share of global retail revenue was largely unchanged during 2010–14, the share of the G7 group of

---

[243] Retail establishments include businesses that sell merchandise, such as motor vehicles, furniture, electronics, building materials, clothing, sporting goods, as well as food and beverages (including grocery stores but not restaurants). For a full description of retail see U.S. Census Bureau, "2007 NAICS Definition: Sector 44–45; Retail Trade," http://www.census.gov/cgi-bin/sssd/naics/naicsrch?code=44&search=2012 NAICS Search (accessed December 15, 2014).

[244] Retailing accounted for 15.8 percent of employment in service industries. USDOL, BLS, Employment, Hours, and Earnings—National Database: Seasonally Adjusted Statistics; figures quoted are for December 2013. Note that many employees in the retail sector do not work full time, so this measures the number of actual employees, not the full-time equivalent statistic. This is explained further and reported in chapter 2.

[245] USDOC, BEA, "Value Added by Industry" (accessed October 28, 2014).

[246] The National Retail Federation's estimates of retail employment are based on a broader definition of retail employment than official U.S. government estimates. The NRF employment figure includes all employment in all economic sectors that contribute to the retail sector, including, for example, logistics, education, and management jobs. National Retail Federation, "Retail Facts" (accessed October 24, 2014).

[247] Planet Retail data, email transmission to USITC staff, October 29, 2014.

[248] The size of individual retail markets are measured in U.S. dollars, according to the Planet Retail.

industrialized countries[249] fell from 43 percent in 2010 to 38.5 percent in 2014.[250] In contrast, the market share of the BRIC countries (Brazil, Russia, India, and China) grew to 27 percent of the global total in 2014, up from 22.6 percent in 2010. China, the world's second-largest retail market, experienced the largest revenue growth between 2010 and 2014: revenue rose by 75 percent to $2.9 trillion during these five years. By contrast, the revenue of Japan's retail market in dollar terms decreased by 11 percent during the 2010–14 period.[251] Overall, as GDP in many countries continued to post positive growth in the years following the 2008–09 recession, these countries' share of global retail revenue remained relatively stable.

Figure 5.1: Retail services: The revenue share of the United States in the global retail market held steady, while revenue growth in China was strong during 2010–14

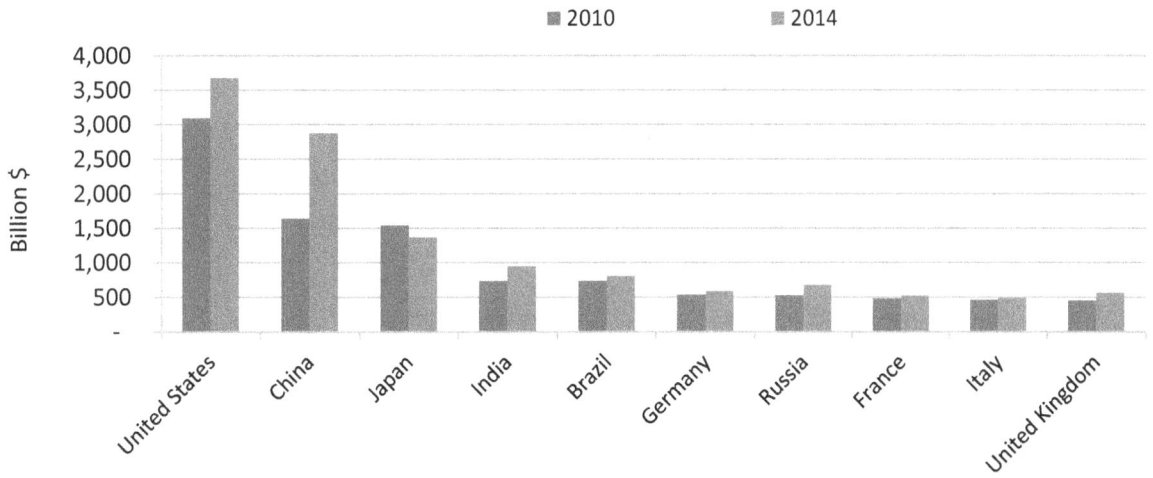

Source: Planet Retail data, transmission to USITC staff, October 29, 2014. (See appendix table B.16).

The world's top 10 retail firms in 2012 were all based in the United States or Europe (latest available comparative data) (table 5.1). Five of the leading 10 firms were headquartered in the United States, and all but one of these generated sales revenue outside the United States. By far the largest global retail leader was U.S.-based Walmart, which operates in 28 countries and generated global revenues of nearly half a trillion dollars in 2012, equivalent to 5 percent of

---

[249] The G7 countries include Canada, France, Germany, Italy, Japan, the United Kingdom, and the United States.
[250] Planet Retail data, transmission to USITC staff, October 29, 2014.
[251] The decrease in the size of the Japanese retail market as expressed in dollar terms was primarily due to a weakening of the yen vis-à-vis the dollar. However, measured in yen, the value of Japan's retail market increased by 6 percent during the period. Planet Retail data, transmission to USITC staff, October 29, 2014.

Table 5.1: Top 10 retailers by global retail sales, 2012

Company	Country	Global retail sales (billion $)	Type of retail establishment	Number of countries
Walmart	United States	469.1	Superstore/hypermarket	28
Tesco	United Kingdom	101.3	Superstore/hypermarket	13
Costco	United States	99.1	Cash carry/ warehouse club	9
Carrefour	France	98.8	Superstore/hypermarket	31
Kroger	United States	96.8	Supermarket/grocery store	1
Schwartz Group	Germany	87.2	Discount store	26
Metro Group	Germany	85.8	Cash and carry/ warehouse club	32
Home Depot	United States	74.8	Home improvement	5
Aldi	Germany	73.0	Discount store/grocery store	17
Target	United States	73.3	Superstore/hypermarket	3[a]

Source: Deloitte, *Global Powers of Retailing,* 2014.

[a] In 2014, Target operated in Canada and India.

total U.S. private sector GDP. Walmart's revenues were more than four times those of the second-largest global retailer, UK-based Tesco. The leading global retailers are increasingly looking outside their mature home markets for growth. Eight of the world's top 15 retailers derived over 50 percent of their sales revenue outside their home country, operating on average in 18 foreign markets in 2013. Several of the leading firms operated in as many as 30 markets that year.[252]

Emerging Demand and Supply Factors

Digital technology and the Internet are continuing to dramatically transform the retail sector. These technologies have given consumers increased choice and buying power in the sector, as they now can purchase from a near-limitless number of online outlets. On the supply side, e-commerce, or online business-to-consumer (B2C) sales, is the fastest-growing segment in the global retail industry.[253] Around the globe, intense competition from lower-cost online suppliers (e-retailers) are squeezing traditional brick-and-mortar suppliers, requiring them to offer new services to meet the demand of increasingly digitized consumers. Consequently, both Internet-based and traditional brick-and-mortar retailers are now working to provide multiple online and offline sales and information channels for their customers. A key technology for shoppers and retailers alike is mobile devices (smartphones and tablets), which have transformed the shopping process to enable consumers to shop and gather information from their home, in-store, or from any location with an Internet connection.

---

[252] Drake-Brockman, "Global Trends in Retail Services," April 10, 2013.

[253] This is in contrast to business-to-business (B2B) e-commerce sales.

E-commerce is Expanding Rapidly in the United States and Other Global Markets

One of the most important retail trends in recent years has been the dramatic rise of e-commerce. Practically nonexistent 20 years ago, online purchases account for an increasing share of total retail sales in most markets around the globe. In the United States, online B2C sales were $226.9 billion in 2012 (latest official U.S. data), an increase of nearly 15 percent over 2011 and nearly double in value since 2008. This contrasts with comparatively slow brick-and-mortar store sales growth in recent years.[254] Leading categories for U.S. online shopping were clothing and footwear, electronics and appliances, and home furnishings. In the U.S. grocery segment, e-commerce sales are expanding rapidly, albeit from a small base (box 5.1).[255] Private estimates indicate that U.S. e-commerce sales will total $294.0 billion in 2014 and rise to nearly $500.0 billion by 2018.[256] As a share of the total retail market, e-sales captured approximately 6 percent of purchases in 2013, and are forecast to grow to 11 percent of the U.S. retail market by 2018.[257]

Globally, e-commerce retail transactions totaled an estimated $1.5 trillion in 2014, up 20 percent from 2013.[258] Similar to those in the United States, leading online categories globally were clothing and accessories, electronic equipment, travel-related purchases (tickets and hotel reservations), and mobile phones.[259] E-commerce growth around the world is being driven primarily by demand from emerging markets with their large populations coming online, including people with mobile devices.[260] The Asia-Pacific region has overtaken North America as the largest e-commerce market. In particular, online sales in China—estimated at $305.8 billion—exceeded U.S. sales for the first time in 2013.[261] In addition to China, which accounted for a 60 percent of the Asia-Pacific region's online sales, strong growth was also posted in India and Indonesia. Leading e-commerce markets in Latin America included Argentina, Mexico, and Brazil.[262] A study by Deloitte estimates that e-commerce growth in

---

[254] U.S. Census, E-Stats, May 22, 2014.

[255] Ibid.

[256] Internet Retailer, "U.S. E-Commerce Sales, 2014–2018" (accessed January 9, 2015).

[257] Enright, "U.S. Online Sales Will Grow 57%," May 12, 2014.

[258] eMarketer, "Global B2C Sales Hit $1.5 Trillion," February 3, 2014.

[259] Nielsen, "E-commerce: Evolution or Revolution?" August 2014, 9.

[260] eMarketer, "Global B2C Sales," February 3, 2014.

[261] Internet Retailer, "How China and the U.S. Compare" (accessed January 9, 2015).

[262] eMarketer data includes Mexico in Latin America. eMarketer, "Global B2C Sales," February 3, 2014.

Box 5.1: Traditional supermarkets are facing intense competition in the United States

Food and beverages represent one of the largest segments of the U.S. retail sector, accounting for over $1.0 trillion in sales in 2013.[a] Strong competition in the food retail segment is squeezing traditional supermarkets,[b] which have been steadily losing market share from 90 percent in 1998 to 45 percent in 2013 (figure below). Three critical trends are driving this competition in the United States (and, increasingly, worldwide):

Consumer demand for higher value and lower prices, with purchases split among an increased variety of food suppliers, due in part to the recession and declining U.S. median incomes.

Consumers' preference for healthier and fresh foods, as evidenced by the growing demand for organic foods.

Internet shopping (e-commerce), which is profoundly affecting all segments of the retail sector.[c]

U.S. grocery stores lost nearly half of their market share during 1998–2013

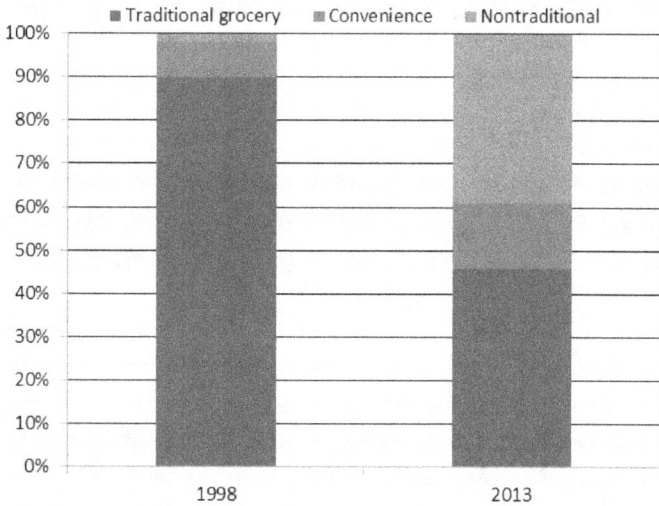

Source: Sowka, "The Future of Food Retailing," June 2014. (See appendix table B.17).

Competition is coming from a variety of nontraditional channels, which captured nearly 40 percent of the grocery market in 2013, up from just 2 percent in 1998. Supercenter and hypermarket stores (hybrids of large traditional supermarkets and/or mass merchandisers), such as Walmart and Target, are the leading nontraditional suppliers. Walmart, the world's largest retailer, is also the leading U.S. food supplier, taking in one-quarter of total U.S. food expenditures in 2013. Groceries are said to have accounted for 55 percent of the firm's total sales that year.[d] Wholesale clubs, such as Costco and Sam's Club, are also gaining market share (currently at 8.7 percent), as are drugstores such as Walgreens and CVS that have expanded aisle space for food products (5.4 percent).

Dollar stores (relatively small-format stores that offer aggressively discounted items) were the fastest-growing segment among nontraditional suppliers reaching a 2.5-percent market share. The number of dollar stores (over 27,000) surpassed the total number of supermarket stores in 2013.[e] Convenience stores, by far the most ubiquitous at 158,000 stores (compared to 26,000 for traditional supermarkets), nearly doubled their market share to 15 percent of grocery sales in 2013.

Within the traditional grocery segment, which accounted for 46 percent of the U.S. grocery market, traditional supermarkets such as Kroger,[f] Safeway, and Giant are also facing stiff competition from a variety of specialty grocers. One growing source of competition is stores in the fresh format category—e.g., Whole Foods and Fresh Market—which market fresh foods (including fruits and vegetables), baked items, organic foods, and higher-end specialty foods. Another is limited-assortment stores, such as Trader Joe's and Aldi, which sell a limited number of low-priced foods and specialty consumables.

A small, but growing number of consumers are also increasingly shopping for groceries using the Internet. This category is dominated by younger and urban customers, who enjoy the convenience of having groceries delivered to their door or boxed for pickup at traditional stores and dedicated collection locations. Peapod, a subsidiary of Ahold (Giant), and Direct Fresh are the largest providers, operating in 25 U.S. markets in total.[g] Amazon and Walmart also are ramping up offerings to compete in this segment, which is forecast to grow by 10 percent annually in the next few years and to total over $100.0 billion by 2019.[h]

[a] This estimate is for sales of food and other consumables in all retail formats, including at Walmart and Target. Inland Institution Capital Partners, "Grocery Trends 2014," Third Quarter 2014.

[b] Traditional grocery stores are defined as supermarkets offering a full line of groceries (including meat and produce), with at least $2 million in annual sales and carrying between 15,000 and 60,000 products. This segment does not include "fresh format" grocery stores, such as Whole Foods. For definitions of the various food retail segments highlighted in this box, see JLL, "Retail Shop Topic," September 2014, 3.

[c] JLL, "Retail Shop Topic," September 2014.

[d] These sales were $565.0 billion in 2014. Leeb, "Walmart Fattens Up on Poor America," May 20, 2013.

[e] Sowka, "The Future of Food Retailing," June 2014; JLL, "Retail Shop Topic," September 2014.

[f] Some traditional grocery firms, such as Kroger, also operate stores in the supercenter segment. JLL, "Retail Shop Topic," September 2014.

[g] Cohen, "Online Grocery Sales," December 2013.

[h] Harvey, "Online Grocery Sales to Reach $100B," November 3, 2014.

emerging markets has outpaced growth in developed markets since 2009. The study estimates that growth rates in the United States (10 percent) and Europe (13 percent) will lag those of the Asia-Pacific region (17 percent) and Latin America (17 percent), as well as the rest of the world (16 percent), during the 2012–16 period.[263]

Despite faster e-commerce growth rates in developing countries, most leading global e-retail firms[264] were headquartered in the United States and Europe. According to research conducted by Deloitte, the top three global e-retailers by sales revenue were U.S. firms. Amazon was the largest global e-retailer, and its sales of $51.7 billion in 2012 were nearly seven times that of

---

[263] Deloitte, "From Bricks to Clicks," 2014, 3.

[264] E-retail firms refer to companies that own and sell their own inventory.

the second- and third-largest suppliers, Apple Inc. ($8.6 billion) and Walmart ($7.5 billion).[265] The majority of e-retailers were multichannel suppliers that also sell products through their brick-and-mortar stores; the most prominent examples are Apple and Walmart.[266] Other top 10 firms included 3 European firms and 2 Chinese companies, the latter reflecting the strength of e-commerce in China.[267] Notably, two leading global e-commerce companies did not make the list of leading e-retailers—U.S.-based eBay and China's Alibaba[268]—because both of these global e-commerce giants derive the majority of their revenue from fees for serving as platforms that facilitate consumer-to-consumer and B2C transactions, rather than from their own retail sales.[269]

Cross-border E-commerce Is Also Growing Rapidly

Cross-border e-commerce (as opposed to domestic online sales) is estimated to represent between 10 to 15 percent of total global e-commerce now and is forecast to grow from about $80.0 billion in 2014 to as high as $350.0 billion by 2025.[270] Factors contributing to the rise in cross-border e-commerce include a general trend toward online shopping, increased demand in developing countries for global (branded) products, wider availability of global shipping services, and surging use of mobile devices to make purchases.[271] Asia is expected to account for 40 percent of cross-border purchases, making it the center of e-commerce trade, while Europe (25 percent) and North America (20 percent) will continue to account for large shares of cross-border B2C e-commerce revenues.[272]

Digitally connected consumers around the globe are increasingly comfortable ordering from foreign websites. The highest such rates are in Latin America (notably Brazil, where 81 percent of consumers reported that they are comfortable with international transactions) and Asia, including China, Indonesia, and Thailand, where roughly three-quarters of consumers are willing to order internationally.[273]

---

[265] This reflects the latest available comparative data. Deloitte, *Global Powers of Retailing,* 2014, G27.

[266] Among the leading 50 e-retailers compiled by Deloitte, 42 are multichannel suppliers.

[267] The European firms were Otto Group (Germany), Tesco (UK), and Casino Guichard-Perrachon (France); Chinese firms included JD.com Inc. and Sunning Commerce Group. Deloitte, *Global Powers of Retailing,* 2014, G27.

[268] The Alibaba group owns Taobao, the largest online shopping platform in China. *China Internet Watch,* "10 Charts to Tell You Almost Everything," June 17, 2014.

[269] Deloitte, *Global Powers of Retailing*, 2014, G27.

[270] BCG, "Cross-Border E-Commerce," September 18, 2014.

[271] Deloitte, *From Bricks to Clicks,* 2014, 3–4.

[272] However, numerous barriers to cross-border e-commerce are hindering growth. These include potentially lengthy transit times, complex/difficult return procedures, customs delays, and price opacity (difficulty determining the final landed cost). BCG, "Cross-Border E-Commerce," September 18, 2014.

[273] Deloitte, *From Bricks to Clicks*, 2014.

Digital technology is allowing both small and large retailers to enter international markets. The Internet offers retailers of all sizes a relatively low-cost channel they can use to reach foreign consumers and to learn about and adapt to new markets.[274] Through e-commerce, firms can tap into existing and well-developed global shipping and logistics networks. For example, most eBay sellers are small and medium-sized enterprises (SMEs), and over 90 percent sell at least some of their products overseas.[275] The global reach of logistics companies and express delivery firms that have knowledge of international markets and customs procedures, and that provide payment, processing, and shipping services, are also stimulating SME cross-border e-sales.[276] Such global networks also boost exports by large retail servicescompanies. For example, Gap Inc. operates physical stores in 40 countries, but it also exports to consumers online in an additional 50 countries.[277]

Mobile Devices Are Transforming the Relationship between Consumers and Retailers

No digital technology is having a greater impact on the global retail sector than mobile devices (smartphones and tablets). The explosion of mobile use around the globe is revolutionizing the retail process by allowing shoppers to access retail services worldwide at any time and from virtually any location that has Internet access. In most markets, mobile devices have replaced desktop computers as the primary channel for accessing online retail sites. According to one report, smartphones and tablets accounted for 51 percent of total retail traffic in 2014.[278] Mobile devices also reportedly had the strongest impact on consumer purchasing decisions, exceeding both television and the Internet as accessed via non-mobile devices.[279]

Although mobile devices are currently used more to access and browse online retail sites than to make final purchases, their use for sales (or "m-commerce") is increasing rapidly.[280] In the United States, smartphones and tablets were estimated to account for nearly 12 percent of total digital shopping expenditures in 2014 and were the fastest-growing sales channel in U.S. retail (with 20 percent growth annually during 2010–14).[281] In many emerging markets, m-commerce is even stronger. For example, in China, $27.0 billion of retail goods were purchased

---

[274] USITC, *Digital Trade, Part 1, 2013*; USITC, *Digital Trade, Part 2*, 2014; Deloitte, *From Bricks to Clicks*, 2014.

[275] eBay, "Enabling Traders to Enter and Grow," October 2012.

[276] These companies include Federal Express and UPS, which offer a range of services to small retail exporters. eBay is also a leading facilitator of retail exports by SMEs and provides a variety of services, including payment services through its subsidiary PayPal. See USITC, *Digital Trade, Part 1*, 2013.

[277] Deloitte, *From Bricks to Clicks*, 2014.

[278] Internet Retailer, "The Ascension of Mobile Commerce," September 2014.

[279] Internet Retailer, "M-commerce Is Saturating the Globe," February 20, 2014.

[280] The use of mobile devices to purchase a wide range of consumer goods is referred to as m-commerce.

[281] M-commerce in the United States increased from just below 2 percent of digital sales in 2010. Comscore, "State of the Online U.S. Economy," September 4, 2014.

using mobile devices, which represented 14.5 percent of the country's total e-commerce sales in 2013. On China's most popular e-commerce site, Alibaba's Taobao, over 20 percent of sales were reportedly completed using mobile devices.[282] By 2017, mobile shopping is expected to account for nearly 60 percent of all online purchases in China.[283] In India, similar high rates of mobile purchases were reported. According to Snapdeal, one of India's largest e-commerce sites, 30 percent of orders in 2013 were placed using smartphones, a 10-fold increase from the previous year.[284] Growth of m-commerce in Brazil reached 84 percent in 2013, one of the largest increases globally.[285]

The Internet as accessed by smartphones and tablets is now seen as a critical component of retailers' marketing and sales strategies. U.S. and global shoppers are increasingly using mobile devices for information gathering and price comparison while shopping in physical stores. According to one study, more than half of smartphone owners, or a third of all adult U.S. shoppers, regularly "showroom"—that is, they examine products in physical stores before shopping online for the same items at lower prices. A 2013 study stated that nearly 60 percent of U.S. shoppers used a smartphone to compare prices while shopping, and nearly half of respondents used mobile devices to search for coupons and read reviews while visiting a physical store.[286] Another study found that more than half of the products researched online were electronics, e.g., televisions and computer products.[287]

The surge in the use of mobile technology in the retail process has required retailers to create user-friendly websites for smartphones and tablets. Almost all of the top 100 global retailers have redesigned their websites to some extent to optimize their use with mobile phones, and nearly 80 percent offer dedicated mobile apps.[288] In fact, website satisfaction is the second most important quality for consumer satisfaction after convenience of store locations and hours, according to a leading consumer survey.[289]

Brick-and-mortar retailers are also developing new ways to reach digitally connected customers, particularly when those customers are visiting their stores in person. Retailers are making major investments in personal or direct marketing to consumers in real time, which is

---

[282] Wigder, "Five Key Online Trends," November 26, 2013.

[283] *China Internet Watch,* "China Mobile Shopping Market," August 6, 2014.

[284] NDTV Gadgets, "Snapdeal Says 30 Percent of Its Orders," October 18, 2013.

[285] Mari, "M-commerce in Brazil," July 31, 2014.

[286] According to one survey, the practice of showrooming increased by 400 percent between 2012 and 2013. Onbile Group, "Statistics for Online Shopping," September 25, 2013; Ninth Decimal, "Mobile Audience Insights," n.d. (accessed October 10, 2014).

[287] Kroll, "The Favorite 50 2014," September 3, 2014; Deloitte, *Fifth Annual eCommerce Assessment,* 2014, 4.

[288] Deloitte, *Fifth Annual eCommerce Assessment,* 2014, 2.

[289] eMarketer, "eMarketer Retail Roundup," May 2014.

now possible through mobile technology.[290] Individual stores and shopping malls understand the benefits of offering Internet access to their patrons and are now providing complimentary Wi-Fi access and setting up Bluetooth tracking technologies to connect with smartphones. For example, the Mall of America—one of the largest in the United States, with 520 stores and 50 restaurants—is installing Internet access to provide mobile-based marketing to mall shoppers.[291] Such mobile marketing efforts include direct messaging and in-store texts to alert consumers to sales, coupons, and other special offers.[292] According to one survey, more than one-quarter of global retailers are implementing location-based marketing in 2013.[293] For example, Nordstrom's Wi-Fi systems in many stores activate apps when a customer walks into a store that provide exclusive offers, along with points that can be redeemed for coupons, music downloads, and other rewards.[294]

Trade Trends

Affiliate Transactions

U.S. and foreign affiliate transactions (box 5.2) have posted strong annual growth since the global recession of 2008–09. U.S.-owned foreign affiliates supplied $101.0 billion in retail services in 2012, representing an increase of 10.3 percent over the previous year and contributing to average annual growth of 12.2 percent in 2008–12.[295] Strong U.S. affiliate sales during the period reflect increased consumer spending globally as economies continued to recover from the deep recession. Although U.S. affiliates' sales were relatively small—just under 3 percent of the value of U.S. domestic retail sales ($3.4 trillion)—U.S. retailers are increasingly looking to foreign markets for growth as the U.S. sector faces constrained consumer spending and intense competition in the mature domestic market.

Box 5.2: Understanding BEA data on retail services

For its statistics on foreign affiliate sales in the retail industry, BEA examines the full range of industry segments, including general merchandise stores; stores specializing in specific merchandise categories (e.g., furniture, electronics, clothing, and sporting goods); and non-store retailers (e.g., telemarketers, online retailers, and vending machine operators). BEA does not report separate data for the cross-border supply of retailing services via e-commerce (mode 1 trade under the General Agreement on Trade in Services [GATS]). Instead, the value of such services is subsumed within the data for

---

[290] Deloitte, *Fifth Annual eCommerce Assessment,* 2014, 4.

[291] eMarketer, "eMarketer Retail Roundup," May 2014.

[292] Ibid.

[293] eMarketer, "Real-Time Data Location," February 15, 2013.

[294] Standard and Poor's, *Industry Survey: Retailing*, December 2013, 7.

[295] The latest available data for affiliate sales are from 2012, while the latest available data for FDI are from 2013. USDOC, BEA Interactive tables (accessed November 19, 2014).

merchandise exports and imports.[a] Retail purchases by consumers outside their home country (mode 2 trade under the GATS) are counted within BEA's travel accounts, but are not disaggregated from other types of travel expenditures.

In 2008, BEA introduced a major change in the way it calculates affiliate transactions in retail services, and revised its estimates of such transactions beginning in 2002 for foreign-owned affiliates and 2004 for U.S.-owned affiliates. Previously, BEA reported only retailers' "sales of services." These included secondary services sold at an explicit price (e.g., an electronics retailer's sales of repair services), but not "service attributes" whose prices are usually bundled into the price of merchandise (e.g., customer service, the assortment of goods offered, and information about the goods).[b] For the revised measure, BEA collects data on retail affiliates' sales, cost of goods sold, and beginning- and end-of-year inventories. It then calculates trade margins that capture the value of retail services associated with merchandise sales.[c] These adjustments led to a significant increase in BEA's estimates of affiliate activity in the retailing industry.

[a] Borga, "Improved Measures of U.S. International Services," March 2, 2008, 24–25.
[b] Borga, "Supplemental Estimates of Insurance, Trade Services," October 2007, 109–10.
[c] BEA representative, email message to USITC staff, February 22, 2010. Data from the U.S. Census Bureau are used to calculate margins in instances where the needed data are not available from BEA's surveys.

Leading markets for U.S.-owned affiliates in retail services are also major U.S. trading partners, including Canada, Mexico, certain European countries, and Japan. Canada ($24.4 billion) and Mexico ($9.0 billion) together represented one-third of total U.S. foreign affiliate sales in 2012 (figure 5.2). Canada's proximity, as well as its cultural and economic ties with the United States, makes it the leading destination for U.S. retailers. Canadian consumers regularly cross the border to shop and are very familiar with U.S. stores and brands. Moreover, Canada's retail sector is generally less concentrated than the U.S. sector and represents a good first step for U.S. retailers entering international markets.[296] Similarly, Mexican consumers regularly shop in the United States, particularly those living near the border, and U.S. retailers have long-standing experience marketing to the sizable U.S. Latino population. European markets accounted for nearly 40 percent of U.S. retail sales by U.S.-owned foreign affiliates in 2012. Leading markets were the United Kingdom ($18.6 billion), Germany ($7.2 billion), and Switzerland ($3.6 billion). In China, the world's second-largest and fastest-growing global retail market, U.S. affiliate sales were $4.1 billion in 2012, up from $2.4 billion in 2009.[297]

---

[296] McKitterick, "Retail Invasion: Canadian Industries," August 13, 2014. For example, Target and Microsoft both opened their first foreign retail outlets in Canada in 2012, though Target has since announced plans to close all its operations there. Hern, "Canada Calls Dibs," November 17, 2012; CBC News, "Target Canada Needs More Work," November 19, 2014; CBC News, "Target Canada Ratcheting Up Its Exit," March 29, 2015. Other large U.S. retailers operating in Canada include Costco, Crate and Barrel, Lowes, Marshalls, and Walmart, among others.
[297] The year 2009 was the first year in which the BEA provided data on U.S. affiliates' receipts in China.

Figure 5.2: Retail services: Canada was the largest foreign market for retail services supplied by U.S.-owned foreign affiliates in 2012, while the Netherlands accounted for one-fifth of all retailing services supplied by foreign-owned U.S. affiliates

U.S.-owned foreign affiliates
Total = $101.0 billion

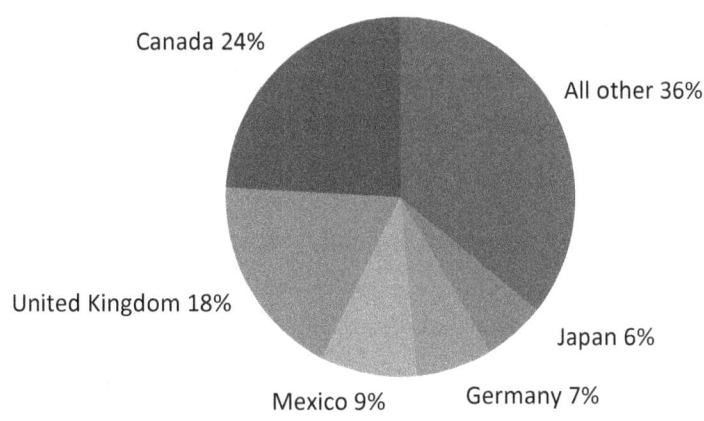

Foreign-owned U.S. affiliates
Total = $43.7 billion

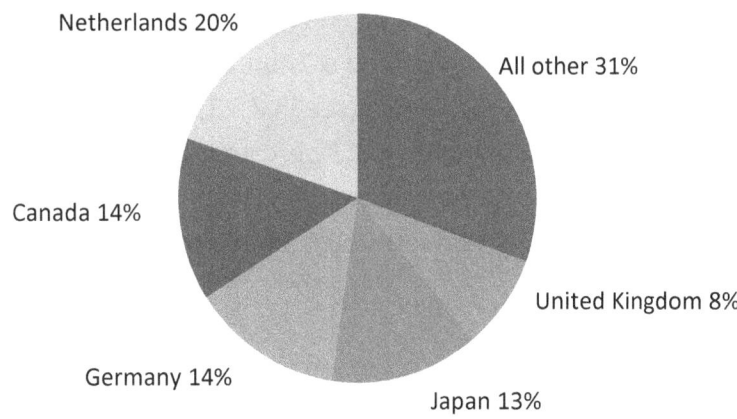

Source: USDOC, BEA, *Survey of Current Business,* October 2014. (See appendix table B.18).

U.S. foreign direct investment (FDI) in retail operations abroad increased substantially during 2009–13, reflecting global economic growth following the recession as well as U.S. retailers' desire to expand into faster-growing foreign markets. Total U.S. FDI in retail services increased from $42.6 billion in 2009 to $65.0 billion in 2013. Non-store retailing operations were the largest investment category, accounting for over $21.1 billion in 2013. U.S. FDI in this category was more than double that in the second- and third-largest retail sectors—building materials suppliers ($10.0 billion) and general merchandise stores ($7.2 billion).[298] The large share of FDI in the non-store retail sector demonstrates the magnitude of global e-commerce, with U.S. suppliers such as Amazon increasing capital investment in fulfillment and distribution facilities outside the United States.[299]

Foreign firms' retail affiliates in the United States supplied $43.7 billion of retail services in 2012. This represented an increase of 6 percent over 2011, in line with strong annual growth of 6.5 percent since 2008. This growth coincided with an increase in foreign investment in the U.S. retail industry, which reached $59.9 billion in 2013.[300] Most foreign investment in the U.S. retail sector was concentrated: food and beverage stores ($24.7 billion) accounted for nearly half of the foreign investment position, while affiliates of clothing stores accounted for nearly one-quarter ($14.2 billion) in 2013.

U.S. affiliates of Europe-based retailers accounted for two-thirds of the sales made by U.S. affiliates of foreign firms in 2012. European firms operate numerous leading U.S. grocery businesses: the Netherlands' Ahold owns Giant, Stop & Shop, and Peapod, while Germany's Aldi owns the U.S. limited-assortment supermarket Aldi (see box 5.1). Japan is another important player: its share of FDI in the U.S. retail market was 13 percent in 2013. A significant portion of this investment was provided by Japanese-based Seven & i Holdings, which owns 7-Eleven. Recent growth in Japan's investment position resulted from the firm opening over 1,000 new U.S. outlets in recent years.[301]

Outlook

Industry analysts forecast positive growth in global retail markets in the coming years. Strengthening economies in developed markets such as United States and, increasingly, in the

---

[298] USDOC, BEA, *Survey of Current Business*, September 2014, table 15, "Direct Investment Abroad: Selected Items by Detailed Industry."

[299] For example, Amazon built 24 new fulfillment centers outside North America between 2011 and 2013. MWPVL International, "Amazon Global Fulfillment Network," December 2014.

[300] During the most recent five-year period, annual growth of foreign investment in the U.S. retail market was 7.2 percent. USDOC, BEA, *Survey of Current Business*, September 2014, table 15: "Direct Investment Abroad: Selected Items by Detailed Industry."

[301] Hines, "7-Eleven Opens Thousands of New Stores," June 24, 2012.

EU, as well as relatively strong output and income growth in emerging markets such as China, are expected to stimulate higher consumer spending globally.[302] Other factors projected to drive retail trends worldwide include the increasing popularity of online shopping, the expanding role of digital technology in the retail process, and contrasting demographic changes in developed and developing markets.

E-commerce is projected to account for a growing share of retail purchases in the United States and global markets. Analysts forecast U.S. e-commerce to nearly double in the next five years to half a trillion dollars, while global online sales are projected to expand by over 18 percent annually, reaching $2.6 trillion by 2018.[303] Mobile technology is also expected to continue to transform the shopping process throughout the supply chain. Projected increases in mobile penetration rates worldwide will continue to empower consumers with a multitude of information and purchase options. Retailers will also increasingly use digital technology, including specialized apps, location technologies, social media, and big data analytics to better understand consumers, connect with them, and offer them a variety of multichannel services (linked online and offline retail services) to optimize sales.[304]

Demographic factors in mature markets, including aging consumers, static incomes, and increased urbanization, are forecast to lead retailers to transform their retail stores to smaller formats and increase multichannel supply to meet consumer demand for lower prices, smaller quantities of goods, and convenience, including store proximity.[305] For example, retail giant Walmart will open more than twice as many small stores (270–300) as large supercenters (115) in the U.S. market in 2014–15, and the company is ramping up its online business.[306] Other retailers are consolidating operations in the U.S. market; for example, JCPenney and Macy's are reducing the number of their brick-and-mortar stores while increasing their online presence to become "nimble" multichannel suppliers.[307] Retailers are introducing web-to-store and store-to-web functionality with "click and collect" shopping—ordering online and then picking up at the store. Purely online retailers such as Amazon are investing in fulfillment centers,

---

[302] IMF, *World Economic Outlook 2014,* April 2014; EIU, *Industries in 2014,* 2014.

[303] Global B2C sales are projected to reach $2.4 trillion by 2018, with annual growth expressed in CAGR (compound annual growth rate). Marketing Charts, "Global B2C E-Commerce Sales," July 23, 2014; *eMarketer,* "Global B2C Sales," February 3, 2014.

[304] Ebeltoft Group, *Global Cross Channel Retailing,* 2014.

[305] Daymon Worldwide, "2014 and Beyond," December 11, 2013; PWC, "Retailing 2020," February 2014, 20.

[306] Walmart, "Walmart U.S. Accelerates Small Store Growth," February 24, 2014. Consumer demand for convenience has also been motivated by the convenience of online shopping.

[307] eMarketer, *eMarketer Retail Roundup,* May 2014.

experimenting with same-day pickup, and potentially opening brick-and-mortar establishments in the future.[308]

Strong economic growth and burgeoning middle classes in many developing countries, particularly in the Asia-Pacific region, will shift the center of global retailing away from developed markets.[309] Growth of the middle class in markets such as China, Malaysia, and Vietnam, among others, will drive global retail consumption in the next 15 years, with disposable incomes of consumers in these countries estimated to reach $30.0 trillion by 2030.[310]

---

[308] Planet Retail, "Amazon Insight Deck," March 2013; CNBC, "Amazon.com to Open First Physical Store," October 9, 2014.
[309] PWC and Kantar Retail, *Retailing 2020*, February 2014, 20; EIU, "Asia Rising: Wholesale and Retail," 2014.
[310] Szakonyi, "Asian Middle Class Growth," October 15, 2014.

Bibliography

Borga, Maria. "Improved Measures of U.S. International Services: The Cases of Insurance, Wholesale and Retail Trade, and Financial Services." Paper prepared for the NBER-CRIW Conference on International Services Flows, Bethesda, Maryland, April 28–29, 2006 (version dated March 2, 2008).

———. "Supplemental Estimates of Insurance, Trade Services, and Financial Services Sold through Affiliates." *Survey of Current Business* 87, no. 10 (October 2007). http://www.bea.gov/scb/toc/1007cont.htm.

Boston Consulting Group (BCG). "Cross-Border E-Commerce Makes the World Flatter," September 18, 2014. https://www.bcgperspectives.com/content/articles/transportation_travel_tourism_retail_cross_border_ecommerce_makes_world_flatter/.

Briggs, Bill. "M-Commerce Is Saturating the Globe." *Internet Retailer*, February 20, 2014. https://www.internetretailer.com/2014/02/20/m-commerce-saturating-globe.

China Internet Watch. "10 Charts to Tell You Almost Everything about Alibaba Group: China's E-commerce Empire," June 17, 2014. http://www.chinainternetwatch.com/7695/alibaba-group/#ixzz3H3w5Qwtk.

China Internet Watch. "China Mobile Shopping Market Exceeded $27B in Q2 2014, 26.8% of Total Online Shopping Transactions," August 6, 2014. http://www.chinainternetwatch.com/8129/china-mobile-shopping-market-exceeded-27b-in-q2-2014-26-8-of-total-online-shopping-transactions/#ixzz3H3tcWl6M.

CBC News. "Target Canada Needs More Work to Get Better, Executives Say," November 19, 2014. http://www.cbc.ca/news/business/target-canada-needs-more-work-to-get-better-executives-say-1.2840913.

———. "Target Canada Ratcheting Up Its Exit, All Stores to Close by mid-April," March 29, 2015. http://www.cbc.ca/news/business/target-canada-ratcheting-up-its-exit-all-stores-to-close-by-mid-april-1.3014178.

CNBC. "Amazon.com to Open First Physical Store in Manhattan," October 9, 2014. http://www.cnbc.com/id/102070643#.

Cohen, Jeffrey. "Online Grocery Sales in the US." IBISWorld Industry Report OD5085, December 2013.

Comscore. "State of the Online U.S. Economy," September 4, 2014.

Daymon Worldwide. "2014 and Beyond Global Retail Trend Predictions." Press release, December 11, 2013. http://www.daymon.com/newsroom/2014-and-beyond-global-retail-trend-predictions.

Deloitte. *Fifth Annual eCommerce Assessment: Digital in the Age of the Connected Consumer,* 2014.

———. *From Bricks to Clicks: Generating Global Growth through E-Commerce Expansion,* 2014. http://www2.deloitte.com/content/dam/Deloitte/za/Documents/consumer-business/za_generating_growth_through_ecommerce_24112014.pdf.

———. *Global Powers of Retailing, 2014: Retail Beyond Begins,* 2014.

Drake-Brockman, Jane. "Global Trends in Retail Services." Presentation at APEC Group on Services Workshop, Surabaya, Indonesia, April 10, 2013.

Ebeltoft Group. *Global Cross Channel Retailing Report: Entering the Omnichannel Era,* 2014.

Economist Intelligence Unit (EIU). "Asia Rising: Wholesale and Retail." Industrial Dynamism Barometer, 2014.

———. *As One Store Opens . . . Retail in China.* Industry briefing, 2014.

———. *Industries in 2014.* New York: Economist Intelligence Unit, 2014.

eBay. *Enabling Traders to Enter and Grow on the Global Stage,* October 2012. http://www.ebaymainstreet.com/sites/default/files/EBAY_US-Marketplace_FINAL.pdf.

eMarketer. *eMarketer Retail Roundup: A Look at the World of Brick and Mortar Retail,* May 2014. http://on.emarketer.com/Roundup-05122014-BrickMortarRetail.html.

———. "Global B2C Sales Hit $1.5 trillion," February 3, 2014. http://www.emarketer.com/Articles/Print.aspx?R=1010575.

———. "Real-Time Data Location Gets Bigger," February 15, 2013. http://www.emarketer.com/Article/Real-Time-Location-Data-Gets-Bigger-Slice-of-Mobile-Targeting/1009675.

Enright, Alison. "U.S. Online Sales Will Grow 57% by 2018." Internet Retailer, May 12, 2014. https://www.internetretailer.com/2014/05/12/us-online-retail-sales-will-grow-57-2018.

Harvey, Katherine P. "Online Grocery Sales to Reach $100B by 2019." *San Diego Union-Tribune,* November 3, 2014. http://www.utsandiego.com/news/2014/nov/03/online-grocery-sales-near-100-billion-2019/all/?print.

Hern, Michael. "Canada Calls Dibs on Microsoft's First Permanent International Store." Engadget, November 17, 2012. http://www.engadget.com/2012/11/17/microsoft-first-international-store-canada/.

Hines, Alice, "7-Eleven Opens Thousands of New Stores, Aims for World Domination." *HuffPost Business*, June 24, 2012.

International Monetary Fund (IMF). *World Economic Outlook: Recovery Strengthens, Remains Uneven.* Washington, DC: IMF, April 2014.

Inland Institution Capital Partners. "Grocery Trends 2014," Third Quarter 2014.

Internet Retailer. "U.S. E-Commerce Sales, 2014–2018." https://www.internetretailer.com/trends/sales/us-e-commerce-sales-2013-2017/ (accessed January 9, 2015).

———. "The Ascension of Mobile Commerce," September 2014. https://www.internetretailer.com/trends/mobile-commerce/ascension-mobile-commerce.

———. "How China and the U.S. Compare in E-commerce, 2010–2013." https://www.internetretailer.com/trends/sales/how-china-and-us-compare-e-commerce-2010-2013/ (accessed November 12, 2014).

Jones Lang Lassalle (JLL). "Out with the Old, In with the New: Why the Grocery Landscape Is Shifting." Retail Shop Topic, September 2014. http://www.us.jll.com/united-states/en-us/research/4959/Retail-Shop-Topic-September-2014-JLL.

Kroll, Karen M. "The Favorite 50 2014." National Retail Federation, September 3, 2014. https://nrf.com/news/the-favorite-50-2014.

Leeb, Stephen. "Walmart Fattens Up on Poor America." *Great Speculations* blog. *Forbes*, May 20, 2013. http://www.forbes.com/sites/greatspeculations/2013/05/20/wal-mart-cleans-up-on-poor-america-with-25-of-u-s-grocery-sales/.

Mari, Angelica. "M-commerce in Brazil Up 84 Percent in a Year." ZDNet, July 31, 2014. http://www.zdnet.com/m-commerce-in-brazil-up-84-percent-in-a-year-7000032206/.

Marketing Charts. "Global B2C E-Commerce Sales Forecast to Grow by 19.3% This Year," July 23, 2014. http://www.marketingcharts.com/online/global-b2c-e-commerce-sales-forecast-to-grow-by-19-3-this-year-44300.

McKitterick, Will. "Retail Invasion: Canadian Industries Ripe for Takeover." IBISWorld, August 13, 2014. http://www.ibisworld.com/media/2014/08/13/retail-invasion-canadian-industries-ripe-us-takeover.

MWPVL International. "Amazon Global Fulfillment Network," December 2014. http://www.mwpvl.com/html/amazon_com.html.

National Retail Federation. "Retail Facts." https://nrf.com/advocacy/retail-facts-and-stats/US (accessed October 24, 2014).

NDTV Gadgets. "Snapdeal Says 30 Percent of Its Orders Now Come Via Mobile," October 18, 2013.

Nielsen. "E-commerce: Evolution or Revolution in the Fast-Moving Consumer Goods World?" August 2014. http://ir.nielsen.com/files/doc_financials/Nielsen-Global-E-commerce-Report-August-2014.pdf.

Ninth Decimal. "Mobile Audience Insights Report Q2 2013." http://www.ninthdecimal.com/wp-content/uploads/2014/06/ND_Insights_Q2_2013.pdf (accessed October 24, 2014).

Onbile Group. "Statistics for Online Shopping," September 25, 2013. http://www.onbile.com/info/statistics-for-online-shopping. Planet Retail. "Amazon Insight Deck Growth Markets and Strategic Initiatives," March 2013.

PWC and Kantar Retail. *Retailing 2020: Winning in a Polarized World*, February 2014. http://www.pwc.com/us/en/retail-consumer/publications/retailing-2020.jhtml.

Sowka, Heather. "The Future of Food Retailing." Future of Food Retailing Report. Willard Bishop, June 2014.

Standard and Poor's. *Industry Survey: Retailing*, December 2013, 7.

Szakonyi, Mark. "Asian Middle Class Growth Full of Promise, Challenges." *Journal of Commerce*, October 15, 2014. http://www.joc.com/international-logistics/distribution-centers/asian-middle-class-growth-full-promise-challenges_20141015.html.

U.S. Department of Commerce (USDOC). U.S. Bureau of the Census (Census). E-Stats, May 22, 2014. http://www.census.gov/econ/estats/2012_e-stats_report.pdf.

———. Bureau of Economic Analysis (BEA). *Survey of Current Business,* September 2014, Table 15, "Direct Investment Abroad: Selected Items by Detailed Industry."

———. Bureau of Economic Analysis (BEA). Interactive tables for GDP by industry, including value added, gross output, intermediate inputs, the components of value added, and employment. http://www.bea.gov/industry/gdpbyind_data.htm (accessed November 16, 2014).

U.S. Department of Labor (USDOL). Bureau of Labor Statistics (BLS). Employment, Hours, and Earnings—National database (accessed November 12, 2014).

U.S. International Trade Commission (USITC). *Digital Trade in the U.S. and Global Economies, Part 1*. USITC Publication 4415. Washington, DC: USITC, July 2013. http://www.usitc.gov/publications/332/pub4415.pdf.

———. *Digital Trade in the U.S. and Global Economies, Part 2,* August 2014. http://www.usitc.gov/publications/332/pub4485.pdf.

Walmart. "Walmart U.S. Accelerates Small Store Growth." News Release, February 24, 2014. http://news.walmart.com/news-archive/2014/02/20/walmart-us-accelerates-small-store-growth.

Wigder, Zia Daniell. Forrester Blog. "Five Key Online Trends in Asia Pacific," November 26, 2013. http://blogs.forrester.com/zia_daniell_wigder/13-11-26-five_key_online_retail_trends_in_asia_pacific.

Chapter 6
Services Roundtable

The Commission hosted its eighth annual Services Roundtable on October 16, 2014. Chairman Meredith Broadbent moderated the discussion in the first half and Commissioner Rhonda Schmidtlein moderated in the second half. The Commission regularly holds these roundtables to encourage discussion among individuals from government, industry, and academia about important issues affecting services trade. This year's event focused on services trade in sub-Saharan Africa (SSA), as well as recent services negotiations and the assessment of services commitments.[311]

Services Trade in Sub-Saharan Africa

Prospects for Trade in Services in Sub-Saharan Africa

The roundtable began with an overview of the prospects for growth in SSA services exports. One participant referenced World Bank data showing that services GDP in SSA has increased, specifically in Mauritius, Nigeria, and South Africa. The participant also cited evidence that since 2002, there has been a 40 percent increase in foreign direct investment into SSA's services industries, particularly in financial services, retailing, and telecommunications. The participant noted that intraregional services trade among SSA countries has grown as well, particularly in banking and telecommunication services. For example, Nigerian and Kenyan banks are expanding into East and West Africa, while the South African telecommunications firm MTM operates in Nigeria.

Following the introductory overview, the roundtable participants discussed the prospects for growth in the insurance, retail, and telecommunications industries in SSA. A participant noted that the "leapfrogging" phenomenon in telecommunications, in which infrastructure development is focused on wireless and mobile communications instead of traditional wired telecommunications, has provided an opportunity for the expansion of mobile payment systems, in Kenya, Senegal, and Mauritius especially. Additionally, mobile applications allow for the development of new approaches for managing activities in a broad swath of areas, including agriculture, education, and healthcare.

---

[311] Sub-Saharan Africa is the region within Africa that lies fully or partially south of the Sahara Desert—stretching from Mauritania to Ethiopia and from Chad to South Africa.

For the global insurance industry, one participant characterized Africa, particularly populous countries such as Kenya, Nigeria, and Tanzania, as offering a significant opportunity for growth. It was explained that insurers often partner with distributors that have routine contact with prospective clients, such as utility providers or telecommunications companies, to sell insurance products through existing mobile payment contacts; the participant described the technique as resulting in "incredible" sign-up rates. Another participant described how funeral insurance is a rapidly developing product market in SSA, since funerary rituals have a strong cultural significance and can be very expensive.

Many opportunities also exist in the retail industry, according to another participant. Since 90 percent of SSA retail activity remains informal, the industry has not developed formal, efficient distribution networks that connect consumers with a broad range of products. The presence of more brick-and-mortar stores, along with modern distribution networks, could also generate economic development, allowing global retail firms to source local products more effectively and connect producers more directly to markets. The participant added that there are opportunities for all types of stores, including small, local grocery stores in addition to large retail stores. Finally, another participant observed that while "tremendous" opportunities do exist in the industries noted above, more-efficient transportation and distribution services also have enabled expansion of a broader range of services industries by reducing transaction costs.

Challenges for Trade in Services in Sub-Saharan Africa

Participants noted, however, that significant legal and regulatory gaps, and undeveloped infrastructure, present ongoing challenges for services trade in SSA.[312] For instance, one participant noted that while contract enforcement is critically important to the insurance industry, limitations in the judicial systems of many SSA countries make such enforcement difficult. Another participant commented that insurance firms tend to establish first as branches in SSA rather than as subsidiaries, noting how important flexibility of choice of juridical form (e.g., branch, joint venture, or wholly owned subsidiary) is for entering smaller markets.

Several participants raised the issue of regulatory capacity,[313] and noted that building this capacity is an area where the U.S. government could provide significant assistance. As an

---

[312] An example of an infrastructure challenge was noted in Burkina Faso, where expansion of the cultural services and tourism industry is constrained by a lack of transportation infrastructure and tourism accommodations. (The purchase of tourism services—e.g., food and lodging—by visiting foreigners are recorded as services exports.)

[313] Regulatory capacity is a broad term that generally refers to a government's ability to effectively regulate a given sector. This can include such diverse goals as ensuring sufficient funding, obtaining training for staff members, and making sure that the agency has requisite legal powers.

example of such an effort, one participant described a project run by the National Association of Insurance Commissioners, a U.S. private body that brings regulators from developing markets to the United States for one-on-one training activities with state regulators. Participants explained that the lack of regulatory support for services industries in many SSA markets is holding back growth. As an example, a participant described the higher education sector in Uganda, which educates many foreign students in-country,[314] but does not provide education services online or establish campuses in other countries due to the lack of regulatory support.

However, several participants also noted that regional regulatory cooperation has produced successes and may be a model for SSA as a whole. For example, East Africa already has a regional program for financial services in place, with other programs in transportation and business services coming soon. Another participant stated that a regional competition authority might be appropriate, as telecommunications services, for example, are often provided by duopolies, with the same firms represented in multiple markets.[315] Finally, another participant pointed out that this issue has gained attention at the policy-making level in SSA, noting that the African Union (AU) Commission has sponsored a series of studies on services regulation and will be discussing the question for the first time at the next AU Trade Ministerial Meeting.[316]

Separately, another participant noted that while growth in telecommunications infrastructure has been high, the starting point for this growth is very low. The participant noted that only 20 percent of SSA's population currently has access to the Internet. Consequently, various private initiatives have been working with SSA country governments to open up more unused telecommunications spectrum for licensed commercial purposes. Another participant noted that in Senegal, for example, information and communications technology services exports cannot continue to expand because of the lack of qualified engineers and training schools to further the sector's development. The participant also noted that support for services trade is not specifically addressed in the African Growth and Opportunity Act (AGOA), and hoped that it would be in the future.

Working with China in Sub-Saharan Africa

Another topic raised at the roundtable was the effect of Chinese state-owned enterprises (SOEs) in SSA on services trade and development. It was noted that U.S. economic aid programs to SSA are constrained by the presence of Chinese firms in local industries, because some U.S.

---

[314] In services trade, this would count as an export of education services—where a foreign student is buying Ugandan education services by attending a university in Uganda.

[315] Competition authorities regulate potential anticompetitive behavior by firms, similar to the antitrust responsibilities of the U.S. Department of Justice and the Federal Trade Commission.

[316] This meeting occurred December 1–5, 2014. African Union website, http://ti.au.int/ (accessed January 5, 2015).

government programs are legally barred from engaging in projects where the government of China is involved. For example, a participant noted that the Overseas Private Investment Corporation is prohibited from doing business in China under 1989 sanctions,[317] and that the prohibition has been interpreted to include doing business with Chinese government-owned enterprises. The same participant noted that as China expands funding of development projects in SSA, those restrictions will increasingly inhibit the ability of the United States to be involved in African development projects. Another participant predicted that as Chinese influence continues to grow across SSA, the Chinese view of how to regulate may become more influential. As evidence, the participant noted that several African countries have supported Chinese positions at the International Telecommunications Union. One participant suggested that, since China is such a significant influence in the region now, it may be beneficial for the United States to work with China on building transparent regulatory institutions and enhancing the rule of law in SSA.

Current Services Negotiations

The second half of the roundtable began with an overview of the state of current services negotiations. The roundtable participants discussed issues surrounding ongoing international trade negotiations relating to trade in services—the Trans-Pacific Partnership (TPP) agreement, the Trans-Atlantic Trade and Investment Partnership (TTIP) agreement, and the Trade in Services Agreement (TISA). One participant began the discussion by noting a lack of progress on services negotiations at the World Trade Organization (WTO). This person said that industry therefore is relying on regional and plurilateral negotiations to update services trade rules and provide a basis for future multilateral progress at the WTO.

Participants identified three policy areas where the need to update trade rules is particularly pressing: cross-border data flows, SOEs, and regulatory coherence.[318] One participant said ideal rules in these areas would include a commitment to allow cross-border data flows across all sectors; require SOEs to compete on an equal footing with private companies; and provide a forward-looking mechanism for regulators to engage in dialogues aimed at reducing the costs associated with differences between national and regional standards and regulations.

---

[317] The relevant sanctions are those imposed by President George H.W. Bush in 1989 in response to the Tiananmen Square crackdown and codified by Congress in section 902 of the Foreign Relations Authorization Act, fiscal years 1990 and 1991 (P.L. 101-246; 22 U.S.C. section 2151 note). Rennack, *China*, 2006, 2.

[318] Regulatory coherence aims to reduce the cost of differences in regulation and standards by promoting greater compatibility, transparency, and cooperation between regulations and regulators. Fung, "Negotiating Regulatory Coherence," 2014; National Center for APEC, *Strategic Framework for Regulatory Coherence*, 2012..

Cross-border Data Flows and State-owned Enterprises

Participants noted the importance of cross-border data flows to a wide variety of industries (box 6.1), and cited the need to include digital trade issues in future trade agreements. For example, one participant noted that the insurance industry uses "big data"[319] in many ways and that the more efficiently firms can analyze data, the more efficiently they can operate. Another participant cited e-commerce and the importance of cross-border data flows for managing the supply chains and distribution networks of large multinational retailers.

Another participant addressed the legal significance of cross-border data restrictions. The participant said that certain countries prohibit firms from sending data to the United States, a situation which can put firms in a conflict-of-laws situation because they are not able to provide the data to U.S. regulators required under the Sarbanes-Oxley and Dodd-Frank laws.[320] As a specific example, the participant cited a 2014 case in which an insurance subsidiary in South Korea was sanctioned by the Korean government for opening its books for an audit by the U.S. holding company, as required by U.S. law.

Box 6.1: Practical problems linked to restrictions on cross-border data flows

Concerns about the free movement of data across borders are not limited to the information and communications technology sector. Multinational companies in a broad range of industries rely on unimpeded cross-border data flows to manage global operations. Cross-border data flows also are increasingly essential as more industries use cloud computing. According to one participant, who provided further details after the Roundtable, three categories of data often cross borders:

- Internal human resources data, which may contain personally identifiable information (PII) and are used for internal management.

- Financial transaction data, used by corporations, banks, and financial advisors to direct the global investment activities of multinationals and institutional investors.

- Customer data, which may contain PII and which are used in customer relationship management and to evaluate firms' aggregate performance and/or risk exposure.

The participant explained that the handling of any data containing PII can be a "flashpoint," raising privacy concerns for both employees and customers. Additionally, localization requirements can undermine a firm's ability to secure data consistent with best practices, as the laws often require the storage of country-specific data on a server within that country.[a] Every server a company maintains

---

[319] "Big data" is an umbrella term used to describe the exponential growth and availability of diverse data sets and what can be accomplished with appropriate analytics. For example, predicting customer satisfaction using text-to-voice analysis of recorded calls to customer service centers. Davenport and Dyché, *Big Data,* 2013, 6.

[320] These are laws that regulate the financial industry.

increases both digital and physical security risk. A more efficient system—one which the participant contends enables firms to more effectively safeguard data—would focus on a small number of regional data centers with a global backup. These centers would be located in areas relatively free of extreme weather or geophysical events that could cause physical harm (e.g., earthquakes) and would allow the firms to better streamline their digital security resources.

Source: Services Roundtable participant, interview by USITC staff, Washington, DC, November 12, 2014.
  [a] Vogel, "Will Data Localization Kill the Internet?" February 10, 2014.

One participant suggested that the general rule for cross-border data flows should be a commitment by national governments to allow cross-border data flows across all industries. Cross-border service providers consider localization requirements, in particular local data server requirements, particularly onerous. One participant noted that several countries participating in the TPP negotiations are also participating in TISA negotiations; measures related to cross-border data flows agreed to in the TPP are likely to be replicated in the TISA. Given the breadth of both these negotiations, the participant expressed concern that a low standard might be adopted in both.

Participants then turned their attention to SOEs, another issue of importance for TPP. They suggested that TPP disciplines should require SOEs to compete on a level playing field with private firms; SOEs should not benefit from subsidies or government financial support. Another participant noted that some state-owned insurers, like postal insurers, operate outside the scope of an independent regulatory authority.

Regulatory Coherence and Domestic Policymaking

One participant suggested that TTIP should be the forum for focusing on regulatory coherence, noting that both the U.S. and European Union (EU) have more or less the same level of concerns, sophistication, and interests. The participant said that the goal of trade negotiations should not be for regulators to adopt identical standards and rules, but rather to minimize the costs associated with firms demonstrating essentially the same degree of protection or safety. Another participant cited a specific example concerning the insurance industry: the EU is currently in the process of implementing new prudential requirements,[321] called Solvency II, which could require U.S.-based insurers to hold significant additional capital unless the United States is recognized as an equivalent jurisdiction with appropriate regulatory requirements regarding firm solvency. The participant said that applying the Solvency II rules to U.S. insurers would result in an inefficient use of capital and would put U.S. insurers at a major disadvantage.

---

[321] Prudential requirements, or prudential regulations, are targeted rules designed to reduce instability in the financial system. *Economist,* "What Macroprudential Regulation Is," August 4, 2014.

One participant expressed the view that regulatory coherence might infringe on the right of countries to regulate domestic issues independently. The participant remarked that there are reasons for countries to make different policy decisions and that those decisions should not be subject to challenge and potential invalidation in trade disputes. The participant noted that some countries' decisions to provide universal healthcare have been challenged through trade agreements' investor-state dispute settlement mechanisms. A participant stated that resistance to regulatory coherence is a tactic used by countries that do not want to liberalize trade rules but rather want to preserve their freedom of unilateral action. Another participant recognized the importance of sovereign regulatory authority for states and commented that the WTO already has a mechanism providing governments with policy flexibility: Article 20 of the General Agreement on Tariffs and trade (GATT).[322] The participant said that similar language, allowing flexibility with regard to regulatory coherence, could provide states with sufficient protections to safeguard their sovereignty.

The Future of Trade Agreements

As the discussion concluded, a participant noted that a forward-looking goal in the area of regulatory coherence is to set up a mechanism through which regulators in various countries dealing with similar issues can communicate as they develop their regulatory solutions. The participant said that this approach could help reduce costs associated with regulatory differences between markets with similar standards. Another participant agreed, but also said that harmonization is actually quite difficult to achieve. The participant noted that within the EU, for example, member states have abandoned harmonization and are now looking at mutual recognition of regulations.[323] The participant further said that future agreements should look to establish a cooperative regulatory mechanism. Finally, a participant expressed skepticism that the WTO will succeed in making major progress on further trade liberalization. The participant suggested that if current negotiations adopt approaches toward greater regulatory cooperation, they may serve as templates for future services agreements.

---

[322] Article 20 of the GATT allows for certain discriminatory measures, including those "necessary to protect public morals" and "necessary to protect human, animal, or plant life or health."

[323] Harmonization addresses regulatory differences by aligning different standards or regulations and requiring identical substantive standards and regulations. Mutual recognition of standards means regulators retain separate standards but agree to recognize standards from other jurisdictions for purposes of importation. Osborne, "Harmonisation and Mutual Recognition," August 29, 2002, 4–5.

Bibliography

Davenport, Thomas H., and Jill Dyché. *Big Data in Big Companies.* International Institute for Analytics, May 2013. http://www.sas.com/content/dam/SAS/en_us/doc/whitepaper2/bigdata-bigcompanies-106461.pdf.

Economist. "What Macroprudential Regulation Is, and Why It Matters." *The Economist Explains* (blog), August 4, 2014. www.economist.com/blogs/economist-explains/2014/08/economist-explains-1.

Fung, T. Sandra. "Negotiating Regulatory Coherence: The Costs and Consequences of Disparate Regulatory Principles in the Transatlantic Trade and Investment Partnership Agreement between the United States and the European Union." *Cornell International Law Journal* 47, no. 2 (2014): 445–70.

National Center for APEC and APEC Business Advisory Council. *Strategic Framework for Regulatory Coherence in APEC: An Impact Assessment of the Dairy, Electronics, and Off-highway Vehicle Industries.* Seattle, WA: National Center for APEC, 2012. http://www.ncapec.org/docs/Publications/Strategic%20Framework%20for%20Regulatory%20Coherence%20in%20APEC.pdf.

Osborne, Kristen. "Harmonisation and Mutual Recognition of Product Standards in Europe: What Options for an Australia United States Free Trade Agreement?" Paper presented at the Australia/United States Free Trade Agreement Conference, Canberra, Australia, August 29, 2002. http://www.apec.org.au/docs/fta2osb.pdf.

Rennack, Dianne E. *China: Economic Sanctions.* Congressional Research Service. CRS report no. RL31910, February 2006. https://www.hsdl.org/?view&did=708785.

U.S. Department of Commerce (USDOC). International Trade Administration (ITA). *U.S.-EU Safe Harbor Overview,* December 18, 2013. http://www.export.gov/safeharbor/eu/eg_main_018476.asp.

Vogel, Peter. "Will Data Localization Kill the Internet?" *E-Commerce Times,* February 10, 2014. http://www.ecommercetimes.com/story/79946.html.

Appendix A
Summary of Selected USITC Services Research

Selected Services Research

This appendix provides summaries and links to Commission reports, published within the past year, that feature topics in services trade, and lists several forthcoming Commission reports that include information on the services sector. With the exception of Executive Briefings on Trade, these reports were prepared under section 332(g) of the Tariff Act of 1930 (19 U.S.C. § 1332(g)) in response to requests from the U.S. Trade Representative, the House Committee on Ways and Means, and/or the Senate Committee on Finance.

332 Investigations

- *Digital Trade in the U.S. and Global Economies, Part 2*

- *Trade, Investment, and Industrial Policies in India: Effects on the U.S. Economy*

Executive Briefings on Trade

- "Nigeria's Film Industry: Nollywood Looks to Expand Globally"

- "China's Trade and Investment in Financial Services with Africa"

- "Rwanda 'Leans In' to Information Services to Achieve Development Goals and Spur Competitiveness"

- "Kenya's Services Output and Exports Are among the Highest in Sub-Saharan Africa"

- "Foreign Infrastructure Service Firms in Sub-Saharan Africa"

Services-related 332 Investigations

Digital Trade in the U.S. and Global Economies, Part 2

James Stamps, project leader
Investigation No. 332-540, USITC Publication 4485, August 2014
http://www.usitc.gov/publications/332/pub4485.pdf

Abstract

At the request of the U.S. Senate Committee on Finance, the Commission undertook an investigation to better understand the role of digital trade—domestic commerce and international trade conducted via the Internet—in the U.S. and global economies, as well as the effects of barriers and impediments to digital trade that hinder U.S. access to global markets. The Commission's analysis provides findings at three levels: at the firm level, through 10 case studies; at the industry level, through a survey of U.S. businesses; and at the economy-wide level, using computable general equilibrium and econometric models. This analysis shows that digital trade contributes to economic output by improving productivity and reducing trade costs. Digital trade also contributes to the economy as a whole as it facilitates communication, expedites business transactions, improves access to information, and improves market opportunities for small and medium-sized enterprises (SMEs).

Digital trade's combined effects of higher productivity and lower trade costs are estimated to have increased U.S. real gross domestic product (GDP) by $517.1–$710.7 billion (3.4–4.8 percent), and to have increased U.S. aggregate employment by 0.0 to 2.4 million full-time equivalents (0.0 to 1.8 percent). These estimates of the effects of digital trade are not exhaustive, however, as other effects of digital trade were not captured in these findings. According to survey results, U.S. firms in digitally intensive industries sold $935.2 billion in products and services online in 2012, including $222.9 billion in exports; they purchased $471.4 billion in products and services online in 2012, including $106.2 billion in imports. Online sales by U.S. SMEs in digitally intensive industries totaled $227.1 billion in 2012. However, the Commission's analysis suggests that foreign trade barriers are having discernible effects on U.S. digital trade. According to the Commission's econometric estimates, removing these barriers would increase the U.S. real GDP by an estimated $16.7–$41.4 billion (0.1–0.3 percent).

Trade, Investment, and Industrial Policies in India: Effects on the U.S. Economy

Renee Berry and William Powers, project leaders
Investigation No. 332-543, USITC Publication 4501, December 2014
http://www.usitc.gov/publications/332/pub4501_2.pdf

Excerpt from the Executive Summary

This report examines trade, investment, and industrial policies in India that restrict U.S. exports and investment, and estimates the effects these policies have on U.S. companies, U.S. workers, and the U.S. economy.

The Commission finds that a wide range of restrictive Indian policies—which are the requested focus of this report—have adversely affected U.S. companies doing business in India. The main policy barriers include tariffs and customs procedures, foreign direct investment (FDI) restrictions, local-content restrictions, treatment of intellectual property (IP), taxes and financial regulations, regulatory uncertainty, and other nontariff measures.

The effects of these policies vary widely by sector. Companies providing agricultural products and food, financial services, and certain manufacturing products, including pharmaceuticals, were the most affected, with Indian policies having a substantial (i.e., prohibitive, severe, or moderate) effect on the operations of between 34 and 44 percent of U.S. companies in these sectors. On the other hand, in some sectors, the share of companies affected was a good deal lower; for example, 7.7 percent of U.S. retail companies doing business in India experienced such effects. Overall, the policies had substantial effects on the operations of about one-quarter of U.S. companies that have affiliates in, or export to, India.

Other policies had smaller overall effects but sharply affected specific sectors. FDI restrictions affected financial services companies most severely, with 23.4 percent of U.S. companies in this sector substantially affected. The IP environment and local-content requirements were most problematic for pharmaceutical companies, with 27.9 percent substantially affected. These findings were supported by qualitative research, including interviews with U.S. companies, that provides evidence of substantial challenges with particular Indian policies in certain industries.

The types of companies most affected by Indian policies are those that engage in a broad array of activities in India. Specifically, large U.S. companies were more likely to be affected by Indian policies than small and medium-sized companies, and U.S. companies with affiliates in India were more likely to be affected than those that exported to India. Indian policies substantially affected 38.5 percent of U.S. companies with Indian affiliates. U.S. companies that provide goods, as opposed to services, via Indian affiliates faced particular burdens: about 61 percent were substantially affected by at least one policy, compared with about 23 percent of those providing services via an affiliate.

Executive Briefings on Trade

"Nigeria's Film Industry: Nollywood Looks to Expand Globally"
Erick Oh, October 2014
http://www.usitc.gov/publications/332/erick_oh_nigerias_film_industry.pdf

The Nigerian film industry, also known as "Nollywood," produces about 50 movies per week, second only to India's Bollywood and ahead of Hollywood. Although its revenues trail those of Bollywood or Hollywood at the global box office ($1.6 billion and $9.8 billion in 2012, respectively), officially Nollywood still generates, on average, $600 million annually for the Nigerian economy, with most of these receipts coming from the African diaspora. It is estimated that over one million people are currently employed in the industry (excluding pirates), which makes it Nigeria's largest employer after agriculture.

Although Nollywood's long-standing "informal" structure and rampant piracy initially helped to establish the country's film industry, these same factors now inhibit future domestic and international growth. The industry relies on cash transactions and oral agreements (rather than written contracts) between local filmmakers, producers, and the marketers who finance and sell their works. As a result, competing claims on intellectual property rights are common, but with little to no documentation, few avenues for legal redress are available. However, foreign observers believe that if the industry were more actively regulated, particularly in the case of copyright enforcement, a million more jobs could be created within the sector. Consequently, the World Bank and private investors are helping the Nigerian government and local film producers to combat piracy and better legitimize its entertainment industry.

"China's Trade and Investment in Financial Services with Africa"
Wen Jin Yuan, October 2014
http://www.usitc.gov/publications/332/ebot_china_trade_investement_finservices-africa.pdf

Chinese financial institutions are rapidly expanding in Africa. This trend responds to growing interest in using Chinese currency to settle payments arising from cross-border trade between China and African countries, as well as the opportunity to serve the banking needs of an increasing number of Chinese firms and tourists on the continent. This briefing describes China's growing trade and investment in financial services with Africa, as well as nontariff measures that could limit Chinese penetration into the African market. Understanding China's role in Africa's financial services market is important for U.S. commercial banks and other financial institutions as U.S. and foreign banks continue to seek growth opportunities in emerging markets, including Africa.

"Rwanda 'Leans In' to Information Services to Achieve Development Goals and Spur Competitiveness"
Cathy Jabara, December 2014
http://www.usitc.gov/publications/332/ebot_china_trade_investement_finservices-africa.pdf

Rwanda is a low-income, landlocked country in East Africa whose development has been hobbled by transport costs that are among the highest in sub-Saharan Africa. In 2000, the government of Rwanda launched its Vision 2020 program, which seeks to transform Rwanda into a middle-income country by 2020 using investments in information communication technology (ICT) services to transform its economy into a "knowledge-based" society. Based on its economic reforms and investments in ICT, Rwanda has recently emerged as one of the most competitive economies in sub-Saharan Africa, as measured by the World Bank's *Ease of Doing Business* index, and appears on track to meet its development goals.

"Foreign Infrastructure Service Firms in Sub-Saharan Africa"
Tamar Khachaturian, December 2014
http://www.usitc.gov/publications/332/executive_briefings/khachaturian_ebot_foreign_aec_firms_in_ssa_december172014.pdf

Sub-Saharan Africa (SSA) suffers from poor road, maritime, and electricity infrastructure. These infrastructure problems increase SSA's production costs, economic distance (or costs of reaching markets), and business uncertainty, hurting its export competitiveness. To develop its infrastructure, SSA must have adequate access to architecture, engineering, and construction services. As many local SSA firms likely lack the capacity to carry out large infrastructure projects, and given projections of sustained demand for improved infrastructure in SSA, U.S. and other foreign firms have a potentially critical role to play in designing, financing, building, and operating major infrastructure projects in the region.

"Kenya's Services Output and Exports Are among the Highest in Sub-Saharan Africa"
George Serletis, December 2014
http://www.usitc.gov/publications/332/executive_briefings/serletis_kenya_services_ebot_12-22.pdf

Kenya is a leading sub-Saharan African (SSA) producer and exporter of services. It is a key services provider to the East African Community, which in addition to Kenya includes Burundi, Rwanda, Tanzania, and Uganda. As East Africa's distribution hub, telecommunications axis, and financial center, Kenya has a broad array of well-developed services industries, with an abundance of services suppliers. These factors make Kenya a promising source of increased services exports. In addition, the government of Kenya is aiming to spur economic growth by promoting exports of services—including professional services, which are critical for Kenya's economic development and also serve as key inputs for economic growth in East Africa.

Forthcoming Research:

332 Investigations

Overview of Cuban Imports of Goods and Services and Effects on U.S. Restrictions
Investigation No. 332-552, *September 2015*

Trade and Investment Policies in India, 2014–2015
Investigation No. 332-550, *September 2015*

The Economic Effects of Significant U.S. Import Restraints: Ninth Update, 2015
Investigation No. 332-325, *December 2015 (tentative)*

Appendix B
Data Tables for Figures

Table B.1: Global services: The United States remains the world's leader in total exports and imports in 2013 (million dollars)[324]

Country/region	Exports	Country/region	Imports
Americas		Americas	
United States	662,041	United States	431,524
Other Americas	243,359	Other Americas	330,876
Total Americas	905,400	Total Americas	762,400
Europe		Europe	
United Kingdom	292,728	Germany	316,804
Germany	286,204	United Kingdom	174,039
France	236,269	France	188,544
Other Europe	1,378,499	Other Europe	1,120,113
Total Europe	2,193,700	Total Europe	1,799,500
Asia/Pacific		Asia/Pacific	
China	204,718	China	329,424
Other Asia	1,011,782	Other Asia	905,276
Total Asia	1,216,500	Total Asia	1,234,700
Middle East and Africa	214,500	Middle East and Africa	410,700
Commonwealth of Independent States	114,200	Commonwealth of Independent States	174,100
Total Exports	4,644,300	Total Imports	4,381,400

Source: WTO, *International Trade Statistics 2014,* 2014, tables A8 and A9.

Note: Excludes public-sector transactions. Corresponds to figure ES.1 and figure 1.1.

Table B.2: Affiliate transactions continue to predominate as a means of trading services (million dollars)

Year	Services supplied by majority-owned foreign affiliates	Services supplied by majority-owned U.S. affiliates	U.S. cross-border exports	U.S. cross-border imports
2005	795,619	571,174	357,017	276,994
2006	889,820	648,286	396,955	313,812
2007	1,019,225	683,840	466,517	344,315
2008	1,116,932	701,589	513,165	380,172
2009	1,071,642	669,342	491,398	355,341
2010	1,155,178	701,185	542,859	377,353
2011	1,247,000	781,551	603,433	404,468
2012	1,292,992	801,921	630,583	422,499
2013			662,888	436,791

Source: USDOC, BEA, *Survey of Current Business,* October 2014, 1, 2, 19.

Notes: Data prior to 2004 were calculated differently and therefore not included in this figure. Corresponds to figure 1.2.

---

[324] The WTO includes the following countries under the Commonwealth of Independent States: Armenia, Azerbaijan, Belarus, Georgia, Kazakhstan, Kyrgyzstan, Moldova, Russia, Tajikistan, Ukraine, and Uzbekistan.

Table B.3: U.S. services: Travel and passenger fares accounted for the largest share of U.S. cross-border trade in 2013 (million dollars)

Services industry	Exports	Imports
Travel and passenger fares	214,774	136,706
Professional services	120,931	84,192
Royalties and license fees	110,781	33,741
Financial services	100,162	69,137
Distribution services	46,627	60,210
Electronic services	51,807	38,152
Other services	17,809	14,653
Total	662,891	436,791

Source: USDOC, BEA, *Survey of Current Business,* October 2014, 1–2.
Note: Corresponds to figure 1.3.

Table B.4: U.S. services: Distribution services accounted for the largest share of U.S. affiliate transactions in 2012 (million dollars)

Services industry	Services supplied by foreign affiliates of U.S. firms[325]	Purchases from U.S. affiliates of foreign firms[326]
Distribution services	399,076	234,960
Financial services	264,466	173,678
Electronic services	99,754	54,203
Professional services[327]	117,662	72,766
Manufacturing[328]	30,788	81,673
Other services	381,246	184,641
Total	1,292,992	801,921

Source: USDOC, BEA, *Survey of Current Business,* October 2014, 21, 23, tables 9.2 and 10.2.
Note: Trade data exclude public sector transactions. Note: Corresponds to figure 1.4.

Table B.5: U.S. distribution services: Logistics services led cross-border exports and maritime transport led cross-border imports of distribution services in 2013 (million dollars)

Services industry	Exports	Imports
Logistics services	23,880	18,203
Maritime transport services	17,175	36.256
Other modes of transport services	4,570	4,266
Trade-related services	1,002	1,485
Distribution services total	46,627	60,210

Source: USDOC, BEA, *Survey of Current Business,* October 2014, 1, 2, table 1.
Note: Trade data exclude public-sector transactions. Note: Corresponds to figure 2.2.

---

[325] Services supplied by majority-owned foreign affiliates of U.S. parent firms.

[326] Services supplied by majority-owned U.S. affiliates of foreign parent firms.

[327] Data are underreported by the BEA to avoid disclosure of individual company information.

[328] Includes ancillary services provided by goods manufacturers, such as computer hardware services.

Table B.6: Wholesale trade was the largest category of distribution services supplied by U.S. affiliates abroad in 2012 (billion dollars)

Services industry	Services supplied by foreign affiliates of U.S. firms[329]	Purchases from U.S. affiliates of foreign firms[330]
Logistics services	19	14
Maritime transport services	9	6
Retail	101	44
Wholesale	238	142

Source: USDOC, BEA, *Survey of Current Business,* October 2014, 21, 23, tables 9.2 and 10.2.
Note: Trade data exclude public sector transactions. Data on logistics services include air transportation, rail transportation, truck transportation, and support activities for transportation but do not include "other" transportation and warehousing services. Totals for foreign-owned U.S. affiliates of logistics services firms are underreported by the BEA to avoid disclosure of individual company information. Corresponds to figure 2.3.

Table B.7: Logistics costs were the highest in the Asia-Pacific region, led by China in 2013 (billion dollars)

Industry	Revenue
North America	1,665
United States	1,335
Europe	1,506
Germany	301
Asia-Pacific	2,965
China	1,593
South America	525
Brazil	285
Other	1,917
Total	8,578

Source: Armstrong & Associates.
Note: Armstrong & Associates does not provide cost data on countries within the "rest of world" region. Corresponds to figure 3.1.

Table B.8: Logistics services: U.S. cross-border trade in logistics services resulted in a U.S. trade surplus each year during 2009–13 (million dollars)

	2009	2010	2011	2012	2013
Exports	18,471	20,592	22,252	22,319	23,880
Imports	15,878	17,951	19,087	17,893	18,203
Trade balance	2,593	2,641	3,185	4,426	5,677

Source: USDOC, BEA, *Survey of Current Business,* October 2014, 1–2, table 1.
Note: Corresponds to figure 3.2.

---

[329] Services supplied by majority-owned foreign affiliates of U.S. parent firms.
[330] Services supplied by majority-owned U.S. affiliates of foreign parent firms.

Table B.9: Logistics services: In 2013, the United States posted its largest trade surplus in logistics services with the United Kingdom (million dollars)

Country	Exports	Imports	Trade balance
United Kingdom	4,078	2,327	1,751
Germany	1,723	1,469	254
Japan	1,475	1,540	-65
China	1,254	1,226	28
Brazil	1,068	452	616

Source: USDOC, BEA, *Survey of Current Business*, table 3.2, October 2014, 6.
Note: Corresponds to figure 3.3.

Table B.10: Logistics services: The United Kingdom was the leading market for U.S. exports and imports of logistics services in 2013 (million dollars)

Country/Region	Exports	Country/Region	Imports
United Kingdom	4,078	United Kingdom	2,327
Germany	1,723	Japan	1,540
Japan	1,475	Germany	1,469
China	1,254	China	1,226
Brazil	1,068	France	1,058
All other		All other	
Other Europe	4,819	Other Western Hemisphere	3,334
Other Western Hemisphere	3,816	Other Asia-Pacific	3,139
Other Asia-Pacific	3,698	Other Europe	2,974
Africa and the Middle East	1,949	Africa and the Middle East	1,136
Total all other	14,282	Total all other	10,583
Total	23,880	Total	18,203

Source: USDOC, BEA, *Survey of Current Business,* October 2014, 6, table 3.2.
Note: Corresponds to figure 3.4.

Table B.11: Logistics services: Services supplied by affiliates of U.S.-owned logistics services firms abroad exceeded services supplied by foreign-owned affiliates in the United States in 2012 (million dollars)

	2008	2009	2010	2011	2012
U.S.-owned foreign affiliates	11,428	16,370	19,160	20,118	19,314
Foreign-owned U.S. affiliates	16,880	14,239	15,213	13,463	13,744

Source: USDOC, BEA, International Data, Interactive tables: "Table 3.1: Services Supplied to Foreign Persons by U.S. MNEs through Their MOFAs, by Industry of Affiliate and by Country of Affiliate," and "Table 4.1: Services Supplied to U.S. Persons by Foreign MNEs through Their MOUSA, by Industry of Affiliate and by Country of UBO," October 24, 2014.
http://www.bea.gov/iTable/iTable.cfm?ReqID=62&step=1#reqid=62&step=6&isuri=1&6221=0&6220=1,2,3,4,5&6210=4&6200=236&6224=&6223=&6222=53,54,56,57&6230=1.
Note: Includes air transportation, rail transportation, truck transportation, and support activities for transportation. Totals for foreign-owned U.S. affiliates are underreported by the BEA to avoid disclosure of individual company information. Corresponds to figure 3.5.

Table B.12: Maritime transport services: U.S. cross-border trade in maritime transport services resulted in a U.S. trade deficit each year during 2009–13 (million dollars)

	2009	2010	2011	2012	2013
Exports	13,603	15,905	16,460	17,055	17,175
Imports	23,219	29,496	31,369	33,206	36,256
Trade balance	9,616	13,591	14,909	16,151	19,801

Source: USDOC, BEA, *Survey of Current Business,* October 2013, 42–43, table 1.
Note: Corresponds to figure 4.1.

Table B.13: Maritime transport services: Japan was the leading market for U.S. exports and imports of maritime transport services in 2013 (million dollars)

Country/Region	Exports	Country/Region	Imports
Japan	2,237	Japan	5,122
Taiwan	1,488	Germany	2,675
Germany	1,382	Taiwan	2,638
South Korea	1,155	South Korea	2,454
China	987	China	2,112
All other		All other	
Other Europe	5,510	Other Europe	14,001
Other Asia-Pacific	1,777	Other Western Hemisphere	3,188
Other Western Hemisphere	1,759	Other Asia-Pacific	2,787
Africa	119	Middle East	928
Middle East	703	Africa	164
International organizations and unallocated	58	International organizations and unallocated	187
Total all other	9,926	Total all other	21,255
Total	17,175	Total	36,256

Source: USDOC, BEA, *Survey of Current Business,* October 2014, 6, table 3.2.
Note: Corresponds to figure 4.2.

Table B.14: Maritime transport services: In 2013, the United States posted its largest trade deficit in maritime transport services with Japan (million dollars)

Country	Exports	Imports	Trade balance
Japan	2,237	5,122	-2,885
Taiwan	1,488	2,638	-1,150
Germany	1,382	2,675	-1,293
South Korea	1,155	2,454	-1,299
China	987	2,112	-1,125

Source: USDOC, BEA, *Survey of Current Business,* October 2014, 6, table 3.2.
Note: Corresponds to figure 4.3.

Table B.15: Maritime transport services: Services supplied by affiliates of U.S.-owned maritime transport services firms abroad exceeded services supplied by foreign-owned affiliates in the United States in 2012 (million dollars)

	2008	2009	2010	2011	2012
U.S.-owned foreign affiliates	10,256	8,334	8,984	9,063	8,668
Foreign-owned U.S. affiliates	3,069	5,850	6,305	6,394	6,464

Source: USDOC, BEA, International Data, Interactive tables: "Table 3.1. Services Supplied to Foreign Persons by U.S. MNEs through Their MOFAs, by Industry of Affiliate and by Country of Affiliate."
http://www.bea.gov/iTable/iTable.cfm?ReqID=62&step=1#reqid=62&step=9&isuri=1&6210=4 (accessed October 24, 2014).
Note: Corresponds to figure 4.4.

Table B.16: Retail services: The revenue share of the United States in the global retail market held steady, while strong revenue growth was recorded by China during 2010–14 (billion dollars)

Country	2010	Country/Region	2014
United States	3,095	United States	3,678
China	1,640	China	2,874
Japan	1,545	Japan	1,374
India	737	India	950
Brazil	737	Brazil	807
Germany	536	Russia	676
Russia	527	Germany	588
France	481	United Kingdom	565
Italy	464	France	523
United Kingdom	451	Italy	492
All other	5,864	All other	7,157
Total	16,076	Total	19,684

Source: Planet Retail data, transmission to USITC staff, October 29, 2014.
Note: Corresponds to figure 5.1.

Table B.17: Retail services: U.S. grocery stores have lost nearly half of their market share during 1998–2013 (percent)

Country	1998	2013
Traditional grocery	90	46
Convenience stores	8	15
Nontraditional	2	39

Source: Willard Bishop, June 2014.
Note: Corresponds to figure in Box 5.1.

Table B.18: Retail services: Services supplied by U.S.-owned foreign affiliates exceeded services supplied by foreign-owned U.S. affiliates every year (million dollars)

Country	U.S.-owned foreign affiliates	Country	Foreign-owned U.S. affiliates
Canada	24,403	Netherlands	8,642
United Kingdom	18,598	Canada	6,215
Mexico	8,991	Germany	5,978
Germany	7,216	Japan	5,831
Japan	5,721	United States	3,686
All other	36,088	All other	13,344
Total	101,017	Total	43,696

Source: USDOC, BEA, *Survey of Current Business,* October 2014.
Note: Corresponds to figure 5.2.

Appendix C
Positions of Interested Parties

Summary of Written Submissions

This appendix includes summaries of positions of interested parties submitted by two organizations: the American Council of Life Insurers and the American Insurance Association. The views expressed are those of the submitting parties and not those of the Commission, whose staff did not attempt to confirm or correct the information provided. The full text of these written submissions can be found at https://edis.usitc.gov/edis3-internal/app.

American Council of Life Insurers (ACLI)

The American Council of Life Insurers (ACLI) is honored to provide our views in submission to your Recent Trends in U.S. Service Trade, 2015 Annual Report. Regarding your inquiry, of particular concern to the ACLI's members are the following:

- **Forced Localization of Reinsurance** – Limitations on the conduct of cross border reinsurance – reinsurance is a global risk transfer mechanism designed to diversify risk, reduce risk concentrations in local markets and provide additional capacity and coverage to local markets often against the occurrence of low frequency high intensity events. Therefore, the changes in Brazil and Argentina in 2012, India in 2013 and now potentially Indonesia and Ecuador not only place constraints on reinsurers business operations but also risk pushing up prices, limiting capacity for local consumers and increasing local risk concentrations. (Attached are two recent letters from the Global Federation of Insurance Associations on this issue relative to proposals in both Ecuador and Indonesia);

- **Forced Localization of Data Processing** – Restrictions on cross border data flows – ACLI believes that all requirements that data be maintained in a given jurisdiction should be prohibited. Foreign companies doing business in local markets should be permitted to transfer electronic information out of the member for processing offshore. Companies should be free to supply data from headquarters, through affiliates, through regional centers, and through third party vendors as long as the data protection requirements of the local jurisdiction are satisfied. Forced domestication of data processing in Korea is already the subject of dispute with several of its trade partners, and proposals in other G20 members would put many global companies in a conflict of laws predicament between their home country supervisor's requirement for comprehensive group risk management and reporting. (Attached is a short Aide Memoire on the subject entitled - "Global Insurance Industry Contribution to Individuals Economies and Society: Why Global Data Management, Processing, Transfer and Storage is Necessary");

- **Reversal of Private Account Pensions** – ACLI supports the implementation by governments of the World Bank model of individually funded pensions managed by the private sector. We believe now more than ever that the twin pressures of increased longevity and lower fertility rates will only increase funding gaps for national governments in both developed and developing markets. While still relatively new in some markets (India 2013) these systems have substantially reduced underfunding of government liabilities and created deep and sustained markets for long term investment instruments. However beginning in Argentina in 2010, than in Hungary in 2012, those governments have forced plan administrators to transfer all assets from these individual customer accounts to Government bonds at an arbitrarily rate. This pattern of de facto nationalization of private savings must be clearly discouraged by the G20, to avoid creating long term systemic risk for the short term sake of current accounts.

American Insurance Association (AIA)

The American Insurance Association is pleased to offer this written submission for the Recent Trends in U.S. Service Trade, 2015 Annual Report.

AIA is the leading property-casualty insurance trade organization in the U.S., representing approximately 300 major U.S. insurance companies that provide all lines of property-casualty insurance to consumers and businesses in the United States and around the world. AIA members write more than $117.0 billion annually in U.S. property-casualty premiums and approximately $225.0 billion annually in worldwide property-casualty premiums. AIA members make up some of the most globally active property-casualty insurers.

Regarding the ITC's question to AIA on cross-border data flows, utilization of cross-border data flows has become an increasingly important part of the global business models of many U.S. insurers as they expand abroad through trade and investment. As a result, insurers note the growing tide of regulations in other markets that restrict data flows and force the localization of servers with concern.

While information technology structures vary between insurers, frequently U.S. insurers that operate in multiple markets will maintain a central data storage server or regional server hubs, and may conduct IT processes from a central data processing center. No matter what the size of the group, insurers that operate in multiple markets consistently see the ability to move data, and store and process it in a location and number of locations that fits their unique business model, as necessary for performing their essential functions and operating efficiently.

For insurers that operate in multiple markets, sharing information across borders is essential for underwriting risk, claims handling, obtaining reinsurance, and performing business functions related to finances and human resources. Insurers need to be able to access operational records, such as applications, policies, and claims, as well as workforce (human resources) data and investment data throughout their global networks. In addition, access to the insurer's data from multiple markets can be an important aspect for systems that detect insurance fraud for some U.S. insurers.

U.S. Insurers

Closely related to data flows, the ability to store and process data in a location of the choosing of the insurer is essential for reducing redundant costs associated with maintaining unnecessary server locations. For a U.S. insurer that operates in many markets, to maintain a server or arrangement with a third party in each market reduces efficiency immensely. Furthermore, an insurer's choice of the location of their central server or servers can be a beneficial risk management tool when it comes to accounting for potential catastrophic events.

The policy implications of the data needs of U.S. insurers are clear. Current trade negotiations and future agreements should contain strong commitments to permit the free flow of data and to allow insurers to store and process their data in a location of their choosing. We appreciate the efforts in past agreements and current negotiations to secure commitments related to transfer information across borders for insurers, and encourage the U.S. Government to pursue commitments that would unambiguously prohibit server forced localization for insurers.

www.ingramcontent.com/pod-product-compliance
Lightning Source LLC
Chambersburg PA
CBHW081351280526
45788CB00009B/2846